ANGLICAN FOUNDATIONS 09

'Sure and Certain Hope'

Death and Burial in the Book of Common Prayer

ANDREW CINNAMOND

The Latimer Trust

'Sure and Certain Hope': Death and Burial in the Book of Common Prayer© Andrew Cinnamond 2016

ISBN 978-1-906327-39-2

Cover photo: 'Face of an angel' © Zweibackesser – Fotolia.com

Published by the Latimer Trust February 2016

The Latimer Trust (formerly Latimer House, Oxford) is a conservative Evangelical research organisation within the Church of England, whose main aim is to promote the history and theology of Anglicanism as understood by those in the Reformed tradition. Interested readers are welcome to consult its website for further details of its many activities.

The Latimer Trust
London N14 4PS UK
Registered Charity: 1084337
Company Number: 4104465
Web: www.latimertrust.org
E-mail: administrator@latimertrust.org

Views expressed in works published by The Latimer Trust are those of the authors and do not necessarily represent the official position of The Latimer Trust.

CONTENTS

1. Introduction 1
2. The Biblical view of the Afterlife 2
   2.1. Old Testament 2
   2.2. New Testament 3
   2.3. Unsatisfactory Alternatives 4
   2.4. This present Life 6
3. Medieval Developments 7
   3.1. The Communion of Saints 7
   3.2. Fragility of Life 8
   3.3. Intermediate States 9
   3.4. Geography of the Afterlife 10
4. Prayer for the Dead 11
   4.1. The Articles 11
   4.2. Scripture versus tradition 11
   4.3. Biblical evidence 12
   4.4. Book of Common Prayer Ambiguity? 13
   4.5. Liturgical Revision 14
5. Reformation Revolution 17
   5.1. Justified through faith alone 17
   5.2. Opposition to Protestant Ideas 19
   5.3. The Communion of Saints 20
   5.4. Protestant Devotional Literature 21
   5.5. The Abolition of Purgatory 21
   5.6. The Homilies 22
   5.7. The English Reformers on Purgatory 23
   5.8. The Articles 24
6. The *Book of Common Prayer* Burial Service 26
   6.1. Having a set order for burials 26
   6.2. Cranmer as editor 27
   6.3. Changes in theological emphasis 27
   6.4. Structure of the Burial Service 29
   6.5. Table comparing 'The order for the Burial of the Dead' and 'The Communion Office,' 1549, with 'The Order for the Burial of the Dead,' 1662. 34

7. Puritan Objections to the BCP Service 35
- 7.1. *The Admonition Controversy (1572-77)* 36
- 7.2. *The Savoy Conference (1661)* 37
- 7.3. *Later Evangelicals and the BCP Burial Service* 40

8. Anglican Liturgy after the BCP 42
- 8.1. *The 1928 Prayer Book* 42
- 8.2. *The Alternative Service Book (1980)* 44
- 8.3. *Common Worship (2000)* 46
- 8.4. *The Funeral Service* 50
- 8.5. *Summary of the Common Worship funeral services* 53

9. The Modern British Funeral 54
- 9.1. *Britain Today* 54
- 9.2. *Practical Arrangements* 55
- 9.3. *Some Principles from the BCP Burial Service* 56

10. Conclusion 59

11. Appendices 60
- 11.1. *Appendix 1: Cremation versus burial* 60
- 11.2. *Appendix 2: Suicide* 64

12. Bibliography 72

1. Introduction

Human beings have always marked the inevitable death of a fellow human being as a significant communal event with a variety of rituals and traditions. Relations between the living and the dead profoundly shape a culture and significant religious change can drastically alter this reciprocal relationship.[1] As Bruce Gordon and Peter Marshall remind us, 'That most reflective and past-minded of activities, the remembrance and commemoration of the dead, is in every age a remarkable contemporary testimony.'[2] Examining how a society views its dead is an important way of viewing how that society negotiates social and religious change and development. This work will examine the impact of the Reformation on traditional medieval views of the dead and how the *Book of Common Prayer* encapsulated these developments, offering the Anglican Evangelical minister today a robustly biblical and Protestant platform for pastoral care and teaching.

---

[1] Helpful introductions include David E. Stannard, *The Puritan way of Death: A Study in Religion, Culture, and Social Change* (New York: Oxford University Press, 1977) and David L. Edwards, *After Death? Past Beliefs and Real Possibilities*, Contemporary Christian Insights (London: Continuum, 1999). Edwards has a more questioning, theologically liberal stance, but his book is still a well-written and helpful primer on the whole subject.

[2] Bruce Gordon and Peter Marshall, 'Introduction: placing the dead in late medieval and early modern Europe' in Bruce Gordon and Peter Marshall (eds.), *The Place of the Dead: Death and Remembrance in Late Medieval and early Modern Europe* (Cambridge: Cambridge University press, 2000), pp 1-16, quote 16.

2. The Biblical view of the Afterlife

The Apostle Paul in Romans 8:38-39 makes the clear statement that even death cannot separate us from the love of God which was so powerfully demonstrated in Christ Jesus. This is the foundation of our assurance and eternal hope. The Bible also makes clear that this eternal life and sure hope is not automatic and not universal, we need to appropriate and take these promises to ourselves through a lively and personal faith in Christ. This is the essence of John 3:16 – the necessary condition to enjoy God's love for ever is individual faith. Perishing or enjoying eternal life are the only options mentioned by Jesus.[1] (John 1:12 is another reminder that all are not automatically children of God, we need 'to become the sons of God'.) Throughout the Bible, in both Old and New Testaments, it is clear that God freely chooses and gathers a people of his own. He saves them and protects them for his own glory.

Immortality is a reality that confronts all human beings, whether we like it or believe in it or not. 2 Timothy 1:10 asserts that Christ 'destroyed death, and has brought life and immortality to light through the Gospel'. Christians can say with joy that they will be 'for ever with the Lord' (1 Thessalonians 4:17). With the advent of Christ, life after death becomes much clearer, though that is not to say that there was no suggestion of it in the Old Testament.

2.1. *Old Testament*

Both with Abraham and Jacob we get hints that they went, not simply to be with God on death, but to join God's people who had gone before (Genesis 25:8; 37:35). All people alike live on in Sheol, whatever the nature of their life on earth (Job 3:17-19).[2] Opinion is divided as to whether or not in the OT there is much evidence of hope after death, rather than mere continuance. However, Psalms 49 and 73 strongly suggest a differentiation between the eternal fates of the godless and the righteous, after the fact that all must inevitably face death. The godly can be redeemed from Sheol. Alec Motyer helpfully sees the progression in these Psalms from present to future to 'afterwards', a

---

[1] See also 1 John 5:12 'he who has the Son has life; he who does not have the Son of God does not have life'.
[2] Cf. Philip S. Johnston, *Shades of Sheol: Death and Afterlife in the Old Testament* (Nottingham: IVP, 2002).

sure hope beyond the grave.[3] Moral and spiritual distinctions are still preserved in Sheol, blessedness for God's people, and adversity for those who denied and opposed God on earth. Ezekiel 3:16-20 suggests that 'dying in sin' is an awful prospect – that is why the watchman's warning must be heeded. Daniel 12:2 is another OT indication that there is such a thing as eternal loss.

2.2. New Testament

In the full light of the Gospel, Jesus himself spoke of eternal loss in the more explicit language of 'eternal fire' and 'eternal punishment' (Matthew 25:41, 46). Paul would take up these references in 2 Thessalonians 1:8 where he talks about those 'who do not know God and do not obey the Gospel', and who would 'be punished with everlasting destruction and shut out from the presence of the Lord'. John in Revelations 20:13-14 mentions 'the second death' as judgement is passed in the highest courts of Heaven.[4] The Bible consistently links together sin, death and judgement. Disobedience in Eden opened the door to death under God's displeasure (Genesis 2:17), or, as Paul says, 'the wages of sin' leads to death (Romans 6:23). Death is normal in the sense of it taking place in the course of nature, but also a supernatural thing, because it is part of a fallen, sinful human being before a holy, sinless God. Sin is a desperately serious and terrible offence against a holy God and results in eternal destruction. The person who dies experiences immediately the blessings of Heaven, or the punishment of Hell, although this will not be their final resting place or state until the General Resurrection when Christ returns and the soul will be clothed again in a physical body.

Jesus was clear that the thief on the Cross would 'this day' be in Paradise (Luke 23:43). (Mainstream Reformers rejected the idea of 'soul sleep', and, indeed one of Calvin's first tracts, *Pscychopannychia (1534)*, denied this purported tenet of Anabaptism.)[5] Calvin, when commenting on John 8:52, states,

---

[3] Alec Motyer, *After Death*, 2nd. edn. (Fearn: Christian Focus, 1996), p 23.
[4] For a very helpful study into the erosion of belief in Hall as conscious, eternal punishment, see ACUTE, *The Nature of Hell: A Report by the Evangelical Alliance Commission on Unity and Truth Among Evangelicals (ACUTE)* (Carlisle: ACUTE/Paternoster, 2000).
[5] John Calvin, *Selected Works of John Calvin: Tracts and Letters*. Henry Beveridge and Jules Bonnet (eds.) (Grand Rapids, MI: Baker, 1983), Vol. 3, pp 413-90.

No believer shall see death, for he is born again of an incorruptible seed. Even though believers die, being united with Christ their head, they shall not be snuffed out by death. Their death is simply a transition to the Heavenly Kingdom; their Spirit dwelling in them is Life because of righteousness, and what is left of death in them is consumed.[6]

Christian believers need not fear death because of their union with Christ. (Calvin's views, see below, would lead many Reformed churches to adopt incredibly sparse rites, or even abandon set liturgy for burials altogether, as what mattered was the believer's soul with Christ in heaven.)

The NT uses the word 'saint' or 'saints' 67 times, but always referring to the whole body of believers, and not a special group – all those who believe in Christ are 'saints'. This is not to say, however, that a passage such as the Parable of the Talents (Luke 19:11-27) does not suggest some form of differing rewards for Christians in heaven.[7] This equality and parity of believers is in stark contrast to the hierarchy of saints propounded by the medieval Catholic Church.

2.3. *Unsatisfactory Alternatives*

Universalism provides a theological alternative to this horrible prospect by asserting that everyone will enjoy eternal life through Christ. Bishop J. A. T. Robinson put it this way, 'In Adam *all* die, but in Christ *all* are made alive. That is the Divine 'nevertheless' beyond all hope, or merit. It rests on no condition of virtue or spirituality, but solely on the

---

[6] Joseph Haroutunian (ed.), *Calvin: Commentaries*, The Library of Christian Classics XXIII (London: SCM, 1958), 201. Calvin on John 5:24 says of the believer, 'But the Spirit who lives in them is Life itself, and will at the end destroy what is left of death... The Point here is that though life in us is only begun, Christ announces it to the believers as their sure possession. Thus he removes the fear of death from them. And this is not surprising, since they are united with (*insiti sint*) him who is the inexhaustible Fountain of Life.' Haroutunian (ed.), *Calvin: Commentaries*, pp 196-97. In his Gospel Harmony on Matthew 10:28-29/ Luke 12:5, Calvin comments, 'Christ is perfectly right when he urges his disciples to despise death, because human beings created for heavenly immortality should trust this mutable and perishing life as so much smoke. The heart of the matter is this: if the believers consider to what end they were born, and what their condition now is, they will have no reason for clinging anxiously to this earthly life'. Haroutunian (ed.), *Calvin: Commentaries*, p 264.

[7] See also Luke 6:23; 1 Corinthians 3:8,12; Hebrews 11:26; Revelation 22:12 for the idea of believers being rewarded in heaven. Believers will also face judgment, but not in terms of punishment for sin, as Christ has forgiven and cleansed every believer – Hebrews 8:12.

unconditional love of God. Consequently, *all* will be raised.'[8] Yet, the parable of the sheep and the goats (Matthew 25 31-46) flies in the face of such thinking and envisages that the future Day of Judgement will be a day of pronouncing rather than a day of invitation. Not all will be saved and the decision made in this life will settle matters for all eternity. God's love *includes* justice, holiness and truth and does not necessarily imply universal salvation. Universalism is also undermined by human freedom. If people freely reject the love of God, are they then forced into being objects of God's loving salvation? In terms of a human analogy, are they falling in love with someone almost against their will? Universalism also makes a nonsense of the biblical teaching above, which talks about the fires of hell and eternal punishment. If universalism is true, no one will inhabit Hell for eternity.

Conditional immortality is different from annihilationism in that 'according to the latter nobody survives death except those to whom God gives life... whereas according to the former, everybody survives death and will even be resurrected, but the impenitent will finally be destroyed.'[9] Both positions 'solve' the problem of eternal punishment, but often do so by redefining terms such as 'eternal' as an irreversible result rather than a state. 'Death' becomes a simple loss of life or cessation of existence. To die is to come to an end, unless through Jesus an immortal life is imparted. Like universalism, conditional immortality sees that if a God of love could not possibly punish people eternally and consciously, there must be an alternative.

However, Biblical Christians would advocate a fully-rounded picture of God's character, his righteousness, justice, holiness, wrath etc., and not just a blinkered focus on love at the expense of all other attributes. If we truly understood the magnitude of sin, we would begin to grasp the possibility, and even the necessity of eternal punishment. The Bible affirms a continuity of person and character after death, and surely that makes sense of the 'second death' in Revelation 20, where the divine judgement means a change of state and place.

Revelation 20 also strongly suggests that death works no moral transformation in a person's character. When the small and great stand before God, the books of life are opened, and judgement is delivered. No

---

[8] Quoted in Motyer, *After Death*, p 29. (Universalism is also intrinsically opposed to election, cf. Calvin, *Institutes,* III.24.xii-xvii.)

[9] John Stott and David L. Edwards, *Essentials: A Liberal-Evangelical Dialogue* (London: Hodder & Stoughton, 1988), p 316.

matter how long the interval between death and judgement, people appear before God as they did on earth. There is no hint of a purification after death, or some 'second chance' scenario, which often becomes universalism. Hebrews 9:27, 'it is appointed for man to die once, and after that comes judgment' again implies that a person's moral state before God is the same before and after death. In the parable recorded in Luke 16:23 the rich man was the same person before and after his death. This has huge implications for how we view ideas of prayers for the dead and purgatory. In Matthew 25 when Jesus is teaching about the sheep on the right and the goats on the left, the same language of eternity is used to describe both eternal life and eternal punishment, with no justification for the suggestion that the ungodly simply cease to exist whilst the righteous live consciously for ever.

2.4. This present Life

If universalism is true, then the greatest display of divine love will be found, not at the Cross, but beyond the grave, sweeping away all human reticence and stubbornness. The atonement is therefore diminished as a result. In Luke 16:31 Jesus makes the point that that if people didn't listen to Moses and the prophets, they won't be convinced by someone rising from the dead. The implication is that if the revelation of God is ignored in this life, no other display will ever convince them. What more could God do than take on human flesh and endure Calvary? John 3:17-19 shows that God was moved by a salvation purpose – only by faith in Jesus' saving work can a person be reconciled to God eternally. The alternatives of salvation and judgement are presented clearly, in keeping with the sheep and the goats, and the Rich Man and Lazarus teaching. The unbeliever is condemned 'already' (v18), showing the urgent decisiveness of this present life. Thomas Tymme in 1605 warned that 'as the tree falleth, so it lieth: as death leaves thee, so shall judgement find thee'.[10]

---

[10] Quoted in Alec Ryrie, *Being Protestant in Reformation Britain* (Oxford: Oxford University Press, 2013), p 461. After Ecclesiastes 11:3.

3. Medieval Developments

3.1. The Communion of Saints

By setting out the biblical foundations for belief in the afterlife, we can see how developments in the medieval church constituted a serious deviation from what God has revealed in His Word. In the medieval period there was a clear, reciprocal relationship between the living and the dead – the living prayed for the souls of the dead in purgatory to make their eventual way, cleansed, into Heaven, and, in turn, it was believed that the dead interceded for those still living.[1] The medieval parish Church was saturated with commemorations and remembrances of the dead – not just on saints' days, or All Saints and All Souls Days, but also for the many hundreds of parishioners or benefactors who gave money or goods so that their names would be remembered on official bede-rolls and prayers said for their souls. These commemorations were woven into the very fabric of communal life, and were part of the great cycles and seasons of the Christian Calendar. Burgess, using a parish in Bristol as an example, highlights the reciprocal nature of the arrangements: The parish benefitted materially and financially, whilst the departed benefitted by having the living pray for their eternal repose.[2] This supposed communion between the living and dead was perhaps the key feature of the pre-Reformation Church. The wholesale rejection of saints, purgatory and prayers for the dead represents the greatest impact of the Reformation upon the lives of ordinary men and women in England: 'In sweeping away the saints, the Reformers had also to sweep away the more humble dead, subverting – whether

---

[1] Protestants would beg to differ with MacCulloch's description of the arrangement as a 'marvellous way of uniting the dead and the living in mutual aid... It gave people a sense that they had some control over death, before which humanity has always stood baffled and powerless.' Diarmaid MacCulloch, *Reformation: Europe's house divided 1490-1700* (London: Penguin, 2004), p 13.

[2] See especially Clive Burgess, "Longing to be prayed for': death and commemoration in an English parish in the later Middle Ages' in Bruce Gordon and Peter Marshall (eds.), *The Place of the Dead: Death and Remembrance in Late Medieval and Early Modern Europe* (Cambridge: Cambridge University Press, 2000), pp 44-65; Eamon Duffy, *The Stripping of the Altars: Traditional Religion in England c.1400 - c.1580* (New Haven: Yale University Press, 1992); Eamon Duffy, 'The Shock of Change: Continuity and Discontinuity in the Elizabethan Church of England' in Stephen Platten (ed.), *Anglicanism and the Western Christian Tradition: Continuity, Change and the Search for Communion* (Norwich: Canterbury Press, 2003), pp 42-64.

successfully or not – the human urge to be remembered: parish regimes were emasculated as a result.'[3]

The physical art and architecture of the medieval parish was also an important conduit through which these ideas of the spiritual bonds between the living and the dead passed to Europe's populace. Listening to the Latin of the Mass in countless parish churches, worshippers would often have stared up at lurid Doom paintings, depicting the last Judgement of God, painted above rood screens, which also depicted the crucifixion. This was a religion, Diarmaid MacCulloch reminds us, 'where death, and the cheating of death, mattered desperately'.[4] Souls were seen languishing in purgatory, others tormented in hell, and still others marching blissfully into heaven, after their souls were weighed by Michael and the angels.

3.2. *Fragility of Life*

It should also be remembered that in the pre-Modern era life was much more precarious and fragile. Infant mortality throughout the 16th and 17th centuries meant that 13% of children died in their first year of life, 9% in first month, 4% in first week and 2% within a day. Death rates were therefore about three times those of modern developed countries and life expectancy was about half.[5] The mortality rates were even higher during the late Middle Ages when the plague killed more than a third of the population in some areas. Tomb sculpture and other art forms evidenced the macabre fascination with the physical stages of decomposition and decay of the body. Even if the Church's sacraments and rituals could protect and ultimately save a soul, the fear of death was still prevalent, but this fear could also have a positive function, helping people to see death as the great leveller and as a stark reminder of their own mortality and the vanity of all earthly things. The *contemptus mundi* of the ascetic tradition and the influence of

---

[3] Burgess, "Longing to be prayed for", pp 64-65.
[4] MacCulloch, *Reformation*, p 6
[5] Ralph Houlbrooke, *Death, Religion and the Family in England, 1480-1750*, Oxford Studies in Social History (Oxford: Oxford University Press, 1998), pp 7-10. In 16th Century Germany the annual death rate was c.35-46 deaths per 1000; when an epidemic struck it could reach 100 deaths per 1000. This was including child mortality, but excluding infant mortality. See Craig M. Koslofsky, *The Reformation of the Dead: Death and Ritual in Early Modern Germany, 1450-1700*, Early Modern History: Society and Culture (Basingstoke: Palgrave, 2000), p 4.

1 John 2:15-16[6] helped in the development of this intense preoccupation with the physicality of death, yet never undermined the potent belief in eternal salvation and the hope of resurrection.

3.3. Intermediate States

Purgatory had its origins early in the history of the church, but was only codified and established in the medieval period.[7] (The Council of Lyons in 1274 made the doctrine official Roman Catholic teaching for the first time.) Aquinas could boldly say in the 13th Century,

> Since a place is assigned to souls in keeping with their reward or punishment, as soon as the soul is set free from the body it is either plunged into hell or soars to heaven, unless it be held back by some debt, for which its flight must needs be delayed until the soul is first of all cleansed.[8]

A huge and very profitable industry grew up around purgatory, centring thousands of chantries and chantry priests, established solely for the purpose of saying masses for the benefit of the dead in purgatory. One could even buy indulgences, or do special acts of discipline to reduce the suffering of loved ones in purgatory. It was explicitly believed that the actions of people in *this* world could benefit those in purgatory, though it was always purposely left a bit vague about exactly how long a soul could remain in purgatory and the exact mechanisms involved. It was, of course, the brazen sale of indulgences in Germany that helped Martin Luther to be convinced that the medieval Church was manifestly corrupt and needed wholesale reformation. There were other intermediate states, or limbo – *limbus infantum*, the state of unbaptised infants; *limbus patrum*, the place where OT saints or Fathers rested before Christ's descent into Hell to release them. Again, the exact relationship of these places in the geography of the afterlife was much disputed.

---

[6] 'Do not love the world or the things in the world. The love of the Father is not in those who love the world; for all that is in the world – the desire of the flesh, the desire of the eyes, the pride in riches – comes not from the Father but from the world.' (NRSV).

[7] Duffy, *Stripping of the Altars*, pp 338-76; MacCulloch, *Reformation*, pp 11-16. MacCulloch points out that northern Europe was much keener on the whole idea of purgatory and heaping up reparations for sin compared to the southern states. This many explain the ferocity of Luther's eventual attack against indulgences as 'clerical confidence tricks', p 15.

[8] Quoted in Stannard, *Puritan way of Death*, p 11. (Supplement of 3rd Part of the *Summa*, Q69 article 2).

3.4. Geography of the Afterlife

The medieval Christian therefore saw the Church comprising of three different levels, or groups of believers: [9]

i. The *church militant* was all believers alive in the present, contending for the faith, fighting the good fight, running the race set before them. (The prayer in the BCP Holy Communion service inserted the term to repudiate any notion of praying for the dead: 'Let us pray for the whole state of Christ's Church *militant* here in earth'.) We are part of the world-wide Body of Christ on earth.

ii. The *church triumphant* means those with direct access to heaven and God's presence, the beatific vision that all Christians seek for. This is where saints, martyrs, apostles etc. go without the need for further purging. Clearly, different ranks and hierarchies of Christians are envisaged – some are obviously more holy than others. Those in the church triumphant were remembered on All Saints Day (1st November). The idea of the general resurrection, where souls and bodies are reunited for either everlasting life or damnation was not particularly emphasised. Yet the New Testament (think of Romans 8, or 1 Corinthians 15) makes much of believers united in Christ sharing a new, resurrection body when Christ returns as judge and ushers in a new heaven and earth. Where the dead reside *now* is a temporary abode until this final judgement.

iii. The *church expectant* was the fate of the vast majority of believers, who need further cleansing and purifying in purgatory before they are fit to meet God. The image is of a filthy peasant with muddy boots, unfit to come into the presence of the lord of the manor – he needs scrubbing before he is presentable. All Souls Day (2 November) was the day in the church calendar to particularly remember and intercede for the souls in purgatory with bells, masses etc., that they may be hastened on their journey to God. It was the solemn duty of the Church militant to pray for and help the Church expectant.

---

[9] Cf. Peter Marshall, "'The map of God's word': geographies of the afterlife in Tudor and eary Stuart England' in Bruce Gordon and Peter Marshall (eds.), *The Place of the Dead: Death and Remembrance in Late Medieval and Early Modern Europe* (Cambridge: Cambridge University Press, 2000), pp 110-30.

4. Prayer for the Dead

At this point, it may be helpful to consider the whole topic of prayer for the dead, which formed such a major part of the thinking and practice of the medieval Church.[1]

4.1. *The Articles*

Article XXII states 'The Romish Doctrine concerning Purgatory, Pardons, Worshipping, and Adoration, as well of Images as of Reliques, and also invocation of Saints, is a fond thing vainly invented, and grounded upon no warranty of Scripture, but rather repugnant to the Word of God.' The Article originally spoke of 'the doctrine of school authors' rather than 'the Romish doctrine'. Hardwick notes that the Council of Trent (1545-63) formally adopted opinions advocated by the scholastics, hence 'school men' becomes 'Rome', thus making the present Article condemn a present, current form of teaching rather than the formal system of doctors. The original draft MS (October 1552), signed by six royal chaplains, included a censure of 'praying for the dead', but this was dropped, possibly in the Convocation of 1562. This does not necessarily mean, *contra* Gibson, that the 'Church of England deliberately abstained from seeming to express any condemnation of the practice of praying for the departed'.[2] The Article does not explicitly condemn praying for the dead, something often seized on by Anglo-Catholics, but it is the clear intention and view of the authors.

4.2. *Scripture versus tradition*

If we stand on God's revelation in Scripture being the warrant for Christian belief and practice and our ultimate authority, then we can only pray for what is included in the revealed will of God. It would seem fair to argue from the silence of the Bible, as there is not a single

---

[1] For prayers for the dead, see Calvin, *Inst.* III.xx.21-7; Charles Neil and J. M. Willoughby (eds.), *Tutorial Prayer Book* (London: Church Book Room Press, 1959), pp 481-83, and W. H. Griffith Thomas, *The Principles of Theology. An introduction to the Thirty-Nine Articles*, 6th. edn. (London: Vine Books, 1978), pp 508-21 for a full treatment.

[2] Edgar Charles Sumner Gibson, *The Thirty-Nine Articles of the Church of England.* (8th Ed.) (London: Methuen & Co., 1912), p 538; Charles Hardwick, *A History of the Articles of Religion*, 3rd. edn. (London: George Bell & Sons, 1888), p 82 n.3; p 102 n.2; p 283; p 410; Arthur Bennett, 'Prayer for the Departed', *Churchman* 81 (1967) pp 252-64, pages 252-53.

command or promise or example in God's Word to pray for the dead. Bp. Christopher Wordsworth in 1873 commented, 'the Silence of Holy Scripture as to the use of such prayers, and the Omission of such prayers from the Litany of the Church of England, are tantamount to Prohibition of them to us, who hold the sufficiency of Scripture, and are dutiful members of the Church of England'.[3] Omission is prohibition becomes a key evangelical defence against those who would seek to re-introduce praying for the dead into the Church of England.

The Reformers were fully aware that prayers for the dead had been a feature of the Church since the 3rd Century, but the authority of Scripture must always take priority over tradition. As Calvin comments, 'When, therefore, my opponents object, that it has been the practice for thirteen hundred years to offer prayers for the dead, I, in return, ask them, by what word of God, by what revelation, by what example it was done?' We 'must keep all our wishes in subordination to the word of God.'[4]

4.3. *Biblical evidence*

In the otherwise very precise Levitical code in the OT, there is not a hint of sacrifices for the dead, despite widespread contemporary practice. 2 Maccabees 12:39-45 does indeed mention prayer for the dead, but Protestants do not accept the OT Apocrypha as canonical or authoritative (Cf. Article VI, following Jerome). In the New Testament there is an emphasis on the necessity and efficacy of prayer in the life of the believer, but not a hint of prayer for the dead. 2 Timothy 1:16-18 has sometimes been interpreted as prayer for the dead, assuming that Onesiphorus was dead when the Apostle Paul wrote, but whether he was living or dead cannot be decided with any certainty. Households can be referred to without the head of the house being dead; separate references to family members does not denote death, merely a separation of distance and geography. Commentators describe Paul's words more as 'a general wish for Onesiphorus and his family', 'a statement of what Paul hopes will be the case for Onesiphorus'.[5] It is

---

[3] Quoted in Bennett, 'Prayer for the Departed', p 254.
[4] Calvin, *Institutes*, III.5.10. Yet, Calvin is not oblivious to natural human emotion when confronting death, 'it seemed cruel not to give some attestation of their love to the dead, when in the presence of God. All know by experience how natural it is for the human mind thus to feel.' Cf. Calvin, *Institutes*. III.20.21-27.
[5] See discussion in William D. Mounce, *Pastoral Epistles*, Word Biblical Commentary (Nashville, TN: Thomas Nelson, 2000), pp 496-99, quote 497.

true that in the early centuries of the history of the Church prayers for the dead do appear, but they are not based on Scriptural warrant.

It is important to remember that the Church of Rome believes in praying for the converted i.e. Christian dead, not the unconverted. Prayer for the dead implies belief in benefit accruing in some way to the believer, but does not necessary imply belief in purgatory – prayer for the dead was offered long before the doctrine of purgatory arose.[6] Yet the clear biblical witness is that the Christian dead are 'with Christ' (Philippians 1:23), 'present with the Lord' (2 Corinthians 5:8), 'with Him in Paradise' (Luke 23:43), in conscious fellowship, and are blessed, as they have died 'in the Lord' (Revelation 14:13), and now dwell in the same blessed state with Christ and His angels (Matthew 22:30). As Griffith-Thomas notes, 'The New Testament outlook concerning the blessed dead is one of joy, peace and expectation; we are to remember their past life, imitate their faith, and praise God for them'.[7] Why, therefore, pray that they may 'rest in peace' if the Scriptures already affirm the eternal repose of the faithful?

As Griffith Thomas points out, 'the root of prayers for the dead is failure to realise what justification means'.[8] The moment we accept Christ by faith we are accounted righteous before God (Romans 3:22), and that settles, eternally our position before God, and our entrance into heaven is secure from then on. *Contra* Roman Catholic teaching, justification, unlike sanctification, is not a lifelong process, but a permanent, once for all transition from the state of spiritual death and darkness into spiritual life and light (Colossians 1:13; Ephesians 2:1-5; 5:8; 1 John 3:14). Purgatory is seen to be required as our sins are not fully forgiven, and our debts not fully paid by Christ in this life. Yet, Romans 8:1 teaches that there is 'no condemnation to them which are in Christ Jesus'. Any belief that accepts any notion of progress and purification in an intermediate state are going against the biblical presentation of justification.

4.4. *Book of Common Prayer Ambiguity?*

Some have sought to show that passages in the BCP are favourable to the idea of praying for the dead. In the Church Militant Prayer, for

---

[6] The Orthodox Church, for instance, believes in praying for the dead, but rejects the Roman Catholic doctrine of purgatory.
[7] Griffith Thomas, *Principles of Theology*, p 509.
[8] Griffith Thomas, *Principles of Theology*, p 516.

instance, we read 'That with them we may be partakers of Thy heavenly Kingdom', and in the Burial Service, 'That we with all those who are departed in the true faith of Thy Holy Name may have our perfect consummation and bliss.' It should be born in mind that the authors of the 1552 Prayer Book roundly rejected prayers for the dead from the 1549 book and are unlikely to have introduced it again in these places – authorial intent is surely against any such suggestion. It is best to read these expressions in the Prayer Book as 'we with them' – we are still here and we wish to go where they assuredly are. In the Eucharistic 'Great Intercession' of 1552 the inclusion of the words 'militant here in earth' made sure that the prayer was restricted to the living. An attempt in 1662 to delete the words was rejected in Convocation.

In the Burial Service of 1549 we read, 'both we, *And* this our brother departed', whereas in 1552 we have, 'that we, *With* this our brother'. The change in preposition is significant, and in 1662 ambiguity is removed with 'that we, with all those that are departed', which is more commemoration than commendation:

1549	'both we, *And* this our brother departed'
1552	'that we, *With* this our brother'
1662	'that we, with all those that are departed'

The Church of England therefore carefully excluded prayers for the dead from its forms of public worship. In 1564 at the service in St. Paul's for Emperor Ferdinand, Bp. Grindal of London noted that some complained – 'here is (say they) no prayer for the soul of Ferdinandus' and goes on to comment, 'in the Scriptures we find no commandment to pray for the souls departed'.[9] It is therefore incorrect to say that on public occasions during Elizabeth's reign prayers for the dead were routinely allowed within the national church.[10]

4.5. *Liturgical Revision*

As an understandable result of two world wars, renewed energy was given over to rethinking the Church of England's denial of prayer for

---

[9] Edmund Grindal, *The Remains of Edmund Grindal D.D.* (Ed. William Nicholson) (Cambridge: Cambridge University Press/ Parker Society, 1843), p 23.

[10] For the efforts to suppress praying for the dead during the English Reformation, see the excellent volume: David Cressy, *Birth, Marriage & Death: Ritual, Religion, and the Life-Cycle in Tudor and Stuart England* (Oxford: Oxford University Press, 1997), pp 396-455. Cf. James Pilkington, *The Works of John Pilkington, BD.* (ed. James Scholefield) (Cambridge: Cambridge University Press/ Parker Society, 1842), pp 318, 543.

the dead in its official formularies and public worship, and also in pastoral care for those who have lost loved ones. Alan Wilkinson in his work on the English Church and WWI comments, 'In 1914 prayer for the dead was uncommon in the Church of England; by the end of the war it had become widespread'.[11] Most Evangelicals did not find offensive prayers of thanksgiving for the departed, the issue lay in petitionary prayers for the deceased.[12] The question, whatever the pastoral sensitivities involved, must still be addressed by Christians in the light of Scriptural revelation. False hope is no hope at all. It is highly dangerous to imply any change of spiritual condition between death and the General Resurrection which we can effect by our intercessions. The Christian hope, as Dean Wace put it,

> is not that his soul will be gradually purified after death, but that, in the words of the commendatory prayer in the [BCP] Service of the Visitation of the Sick, it may, in death itself, be washed in the blood of that immaculate Lamb, and presented, when it leaves the body, 'pure and without spot' unto God. Prayers, in short, which have any tinge of a purgatorial view are unauthorised by Scripture, and inconsistent with a most blessed element of Evangelical hope and faith.[13]

Advocates for liturgical reform pointed out that although official teaching omitted prayers for the dead, the practice was commonplace in private devotions, with Lancelot Andrewes 'Private Devotions' (first published 1648) often held up as an example. Any distinction between private and public prayers is surely unhelpful – if it is against the teaching of Scripture and therefore inadmissible in one sphere, then surely that is so in the other sphere? Can one with any integrity allow something in private, yet condemn it in public?

---

[11] Quoted in 'Can we pray for the dead?' by Andrew Goddard, http://www.fulcrum-anglican.org.uk/articles/can-we-pray-for-the-dead/. Goddard was particularly looking at the resources produced by the Church of England for the centenary of the start of WWI. They mark a radical departure from the Reformed doctrine of the Church of English formularies, with, for example praying indiscriminately for the fallen, whether 'in Christ' or not. A universalist thinking begins to creep in. Again, prayers that are not authorised have been made available for public use. Accessed 18 November 2015.

[12] For vexed questions of Anglican liturgical revision, see H. R. M. Craig, 'Prayer and the Departed', *Churchman* 86 (1972) pp 201-04; Bennett, 'Prayer for the Departed'; David Phillips, 'What should we pray? Prayer for the dead in Anglican liturgy', *Crossway* Autumn (2007).

[13] Quoted in Griffith Thomas, *Principles of Theology*, p 520.

The proposed 1928 BCP re-introduced All Souls into the Calendar with a Collect. Lowther Clarke, a proponent of the changes, commented,

> Prayers for the Dead, it may be argued, are excluded from the public services of the Reformed Church of England, or at most merely hinted at in ambiguous language; in thus sanctioning them the new book upsets the existing doctrinal balance. The best answer is that a revised Prayer Book must to a large extent register the changes which have gradually taken place in religious practice. Prayers for the Departed – this is a better phrase, because we pray not for the *dead* but for those who are alive in God – are now used so widely by Churchmen of all schools of thought that a book intended for Churchmen must recognise them. No one could maintain that they are wrong; the most that can be said is that we have no ground for believing them to have any effect. That is to say, while many believe them to be an indispensable, or at least a highly desirable, part of Christian devotion, some consider them unnecessary, but harmless. Clearly the reasons for their inclusion are very strong.[14]

Opposing the revisions, Joynson-Hicks insisted that the introduction of the celebration of All Souls, 'a festival from the Roman Calendar which is rooted in the Romish doctrine of purgatory, taken in conjunction with the provision for Requiem celebrations, really Requiem Masses, goes a long way to re-establish the doctrine of Purgatory in the English Church'.[15]

---

[14] W. K. Lowther Clarke, *The New Prayer Book Explained*, rev. edn. (London: SPCK, 1927), pp 12-13.

[15] William Joynson-Hicks, *The Prayer Book Crisis* (London: Putnam, 1928), pp 133-34.

5. Reformation Revolution

5.1. *Justified through faith alone*

The Reformation represented a huge challenge to centuries-old beliefs and practices about death and burial in the Church. The Protestant doctrine of justification by faith alone meant that every soul had to deal with God themselves without the need for any intermediaries, Mary, the saints, or even the ministrations of the Church itself, was unnecessary. Chantries were therefore unnecessary and to be dissolved, as was the cult of Mary and the saints. The evidence of wills after the Reformation shows that for Protestants the first bequest of the testator's soul was no longer to Mary and the saints, but to the merits of Christ alone.[1] Luther said in the 13th of his 95 Theses that 'the dying will pay all their debts by their death', in other words, the whole theory of satisfactions and pardons was redundant when we could be assured of salvation in this life.[2] Melanchthon was very clear on the momentous import of the doctrine:

> Let those who marvel that justification is attributed only to faith alone marvel also that justification is attributed only to the mercy of God, and not rather to human merits... wherever you turn, whether to the works preceding justification, or to those that follow, there is no room for our merit'.[3]

We are pronounced righteous by trusting in God's mercy alone. We are therefore clothed in an alien, extrinsic righteousness, which removes divine judgement.

Grace was redefined not as something we have or store up, but as God's favour to us. Euan Cameron helpfully describes just how radical this change in thinking was:

> This teaching overturned the very basis in which the medieval pastoral cycle of sin, confession, and absolution rested. Both the theoretical and the pastoral theology of the late middle ages had

---

[1] For the debate on using wills to gauge religious affiliation, see MacCulloch, *Reformation*, pp 576, 764 n.1.

[2] Euan Cameron, *The European Reformation*, 2nd. edn. (Oxford: Oxford University Press, 2012), 154. For a fuller treatment of Luther on death and eternity, see Paul Althaus, *The Theology of Martin Luther* (Philadelphia: Fortress Press, 1966), pp 404-25.

[3] Quoted in Euan Cameron, *The European Reformation* (Oxford: The Clarendon Press, 2000), p 122. See also Calvin, *Institutes* III.xi.2.

assumed that the believer would alternate between sin and grace, passing from the former to the latter through the sacraments of penance and communion. By this medieval wisdom, a man was sometimes a sinner, sometimes righteous – but never both at the same time. For the reformers, on the other hand, the oscillating cycle of sin and 'grace' was meaningless: in Luther's phrase [*simul justus et peccator*], a believer was at one and the same time a sinner and a righteous man: a sinner in respect of his actual conduct, but justified or 'righteous' inasmuch as God gratuitously attributed Christ's merits to him.[4]

Luther shocked his Wittenberg congregation in 1522 by emphasising the isolation of death:

> The summons of death comes to us all, and no one can die for another. Everyone must fight his own battle with death by himself, alone. We can shout into each other's ears, but everyone must himself be prepared for the time of death: I will not be with you then, nor you with me.[5]

The theological revolution in justification by faith alone meant that the very foundations of much of medieval Catholicism were torn down. As Eamon Duffy, the doyen of revisionist thinking on the English Reformation, comments, 'The [Communion] service was no longer a rite of intercession on behalf of the dead, but an exhortation to faith on the part of the living... the boundaries of human community have been redrawn'.[6] And as Alister McGrath puts it, 'the conceptual glue binding the church's rites, ceremonies, institutions, and ideas was fatally weakened... the church would now play a subsidiary role in the dispensation of salvation, subordinate to the direct encounter between the individual human being and God'.[7] The living could not alter the fate of the dead; the individual's decisions on earth determined where they would spend eternity. The Church's teaching on satisfactions, saying masses for the dead, indulgences etc. was rejected in Protestant belief. For millions of people in Europe this was perhaps the greatest upheaval of the Reformation, but it raised disturbing questions: Were they now dishonouring the dead and condemning them to torment?

---

[4] Euan Cameron, *The European Reformation*, p 123.
[5] Quoted in Koslofsky, *The Reformation of the Dead*, p 3.
[6] Duffy, *Stripping of the Altars*, p 475.
[7] Alister McGrath, *Christianity's Dangerous Idea: The Protestant Revolution. A History from the sixteenth century to the twenty-first.* (London: SPCK, 2007), pp 43-44.

Maybe it would lead to countless lost souls visiting the living as ghosts? What about all the money that had already been paid to chantries, fraternities etc?[8]

5.2. Opposition to Protestant Ideas

Despite official Protestant theology, the idea of the bond between the living and the departed was too deeply-rooted to be easily eradicated. Ronald Hutton has drawn attention to just how resistant parishes were to stop ringing church bells on All Saints' Night, which was believed to comfort the souls of the dead and ease their spiritual wanderings. Despite countless visitations and injunctions they were still being rung well into the 17th Century. Hutton points out that the tradition lasted so long as it did not need illegal ornaments or a priest, and could be carried out after dark.[9] (On 27th September 1573 the consistory of Naaldwijk, Holland decided 'that henceforth the bell shall, for the time being, not be rung at the burial of the dead in order to remove from men's hearts the abominable superstition of the Papists, who believe and teach that the ringing confers benefit to the dead.'[10])

MacDonald and Murphy talk of 'the Protestant goal of demystifying space', where no particular part of the church building or churchyard was now seen as holier than another. The north side of the churchyard had been traditionally dreaded, being reserved for the unbaptised, excommunicants and suicides.[11] It was widely held that burials in a church would be more efficacious the closer they were to chancel and altar. Protestant beliefs had very concrete and practical implications in the lives of many people, and ancient customs were hard to eradicate, as

---

[8] The Zurich theologian Ludwig Lavater mocked the traditional belief that ghosts might be souls of the dead allowed to leave purgatory to seek prayers and intercessory masses. Lavater's work *On Spectres* was published in German in 1569, in Latin in 1570, and in English in 1596. Cf. Bruce Gordon, 'Malevolent ghosts and ministering angels: apparitions and pastoral care in the Swiss Reformation' in Bruce Gordon and Peter Marshall (eds.), *The Place of the Dead: Death and Remembrance in Late Medieval and Early Modern Europe* (Cambridge: Cambridge University Press, 2000), pp 87-109; Cameron, *The European Reformation*, pp 425, 550 n. 141.

[9] Ronald Hutton, *The Rise and Fall of Merry England: The Ritual Year 1400-1700* (Oxford: Oxford University Press, 1994), pp 106-7.

[10] Alastair Duke, Gillian Lewis and Andrew Pettegree (eds.), *Calvinism in Europe, 1540-1610: A collection of Documents* (Manchester: Manchester University Press, 1992), p 167.

[11] Michael MacDonald and Terence R. Murphy, *Sleepless Souls: Suicide in Early Modern England*, Oxford Studies in Social History (Oxford: Oxford University Press, 1990), p 46.

5.3. The Communion of Saints

evidenced by the often exasperated records of bishops' injunctions and visitations in their dioceses.

The 'Communion of the saints' (*communio sanctorum*) originally referred to the close bond and reciprocal link between the living and the dead.[12] Reformers such as Luther (*Sermons on the Catechism*, 1528) preferred to speak of the communion in terms of the true Church, which consists of believers both militant on earth and triumphant in heaven, but with no reference to intercession for the dead. 'Saints' were now to be seen as all true believers; specially favoured believers were in no sense meritorious or intercessors for the living. The Apostles' Creed, which has the communion of saints as an article of faith, therefore needed to be read in a different way – now, with the church expectant removed, and the church triumphant linked with Christians here on earth, the church militant. Martin Bucer comments,

> We teach that the blessed saints who lie in the presence of our Lord Christ and of whose lives we have biblical or other trustworthy accounts, ought to be commemorated in such a way, that the congregation is shown what graces and gifts their God and Father and ours conferred upon them through our common Saviour and that we should give thanks to God for them, and rejoice with them as members of one body over those graces and gifts, so that we may be strongly provoked to place greater confidence in the grace of God for ourselves, and to follow the example of their faith.[13]

This is in tune with the prayer in the BCP Holy Communion service:

> And we also bless thy holy Name for all thy servants departed this life in thy faith and fear; beseeching thee to give us grace so to follow their good examples, that with them we may be partakers of thy heavenly kingdom.

The faithful dead are no longer to be prayed for, but to be given thanks for, and their examples followed.

---

[12] Cameron, *The European Reformation*, pp 93, 161, 172-73; for cult of the saints, pp 18-21.
[13] Quoted in N. T. Wright, *For all the Saints? Remembering the Christian Departed* (London: SPCK, 2003), p 38.

5.4. *Protestant Devotional Literature*

In a move away from a more sacramental form of ministry during death and burial, Protestants had to develop new forms of ministry and pastoral care, often censoring traditional Catholic works. Protestant writers such as Thomas Becon and William Perkins produced works to ease the troubled conscience and replace the medieval *ars moriendi* ('Art of Dying') with works based firmly on acceptable Reformation theology.[14] 'Dying well' meant being an edifying witness to Christ and example to others, which often included having family and friends gathered around the death-bed to hear the last words of a dying man or woman, and to offer comfort and help when necessary. A dying individual giving a reason for their confidence in Christ's saving work on the Cross to enter heaven confidently was seen as a powerful and much lauded witness to both God and others.

> A large body of surviving evidence leaves no doubt that believers were buoyed up in the face of physical extinction, and supported through appalling pain, by the prospect of eternal life. The enormous early-modern interest in death-bed performances may seem morbid to us with our very different attitudes and perspective. But this interest had very little of the mawkish sentimentality which early twentieth-century sensibilities detected in Victorian death-bed literature. At issue were life and death: eternal life or the living death of the soul.[15]

5.5. *The Abolition of Purgatory*

When purgatory was officially excised from Church of England formularies, leaving the binary options of heaven and hell as the only options in the afterlife, people also began to ask wider questions about the geographical realities of heaven and hell. As Peter Marshall puts it, 'distinct cracks in the edifice of conventional belief about a localised afterlife can be detected spreading slowly...'[16] To many it seemed that once you began to unpick some elements of traditional religion, such as

---

[14] Mary Hampson Patterson, *Domesticating the Reformation: Protestant Best Sellers, Private Devotion, and the Revolution of English Piety* (Madison, NJ: Fairleigh Dickinson University Press, 2007).

[15] Ralph Houlbrooke, 'The Puritan Death-bed, c.1560- c.1660' in Christopher Durston and Jacqueline Eales (eds.), *The Culture of English Puritanism, 1560-1700* (Basingstoke: Macmillan, 1996), pp 122-44, quotation 142.

[16] Marshall, "The map of God's word", quote 111.

purgatory and prayers for the dead, then the whole spiritual garment could unravel, and, indeed, more radical voices could be heard from the time of the break with Rome to the confusion of the English Civil War.

John Jewel mockingly referred to the papists' 'lists and gainful territories of Purgatory' and the medieval flights of fancy imagining the landscapes of the afterlife.[17] Although Protestant polemicists enjoyed mocking Roman Catholic ideas of Purgatory, Protestants themselves were soon engaged in literary controversy over Christ's descent into Hell and the notion of 'soul sleep'.[18] Both of these debates touched on the geography and material location of the afterlife. Protestants could laugh at Romish ideas of where souls resided, but could be divided amongst themselves on the same sort of issues. There were also debates centring around 'Abraham's bosom' and where Lazarus had been for four days before being resuscitated by Christ. Many simply asserted that it was unwise to be dogmatic on the location of Hell, when the Scriptures did not give a clear picture. A 'reverential agnosticism' therefore developed across the confessional spectrum.[19] As early as 1550 Roger Hutchinson complained of 'Libertines' who denied the reality of Heaven and Hell and that Hell was 'nothing but a tormenting and desperate conscience'.[20] The crude geographical terms of the Middle Ages could give way to equally unscriptural and rationalistic ideas of heaven and hell only understood in symbolic or metaphorical terms, bypassing more balanced, biblical conceptions. Questioning purgatory could also mean questioning any afterlife at all.

5.6. The Homilies

The Homily Concerning Prayer (probably by John Jewel), reflecting on the parable of the Rich Man and Lazarus in Luke 16, speaks clearly of the needlessness of praying for the dead: 'the sentence of God is unchangeable, and cannot be revoked again. Therefore let us not deceive ourselves, thinking that either we may help others, or others may help us by their good and charitable prayers in time to come.' The author also cites John 3:36 and Ecclesiastes 11:3 to reinforce his point

---

[17] John Jewel, *The Works of John Jewel*. John Ayre (ed.) (Cambridge: Parker Society/ Cambridge University Press, 1845-1850), Vol. 4, p 845. For other Protestant polemics on the theme, see Marshall, "The map of God's word", pp 114-15.
[18] Peter Milward, *Religious Controversies of the Elizabethan Age: A Survey of Printed Sources* (Lincoln, Neb. ; London: University of Nebraska Press, 1977). See Appendix 2.
[19] Marshall, "The map of God's word", p 120.
[20] Quoted in Marshall, "The map of God's word", p 127.

and also marshals Augustine, Chrysostom and Cyprian to his cause that 'when they are once departed out of this life, there is no place for repentance, nor yet for satisfaction'.[21] The blood of Christ is uniquely and completely sufficient to purge the guilty sinner (1 John 1:9; Hebrews 9:14; 10:10,14). This becomes the key Protestant argument against Purgatory. The author affirms that, 'The only purgatory wherein we must trust to be saved is the death and blood of Christ, which if we apprehend with a true and steadfast faith, it purgeth and cleanseth us from all our sins.' Mentioning 1 John 2:1, [My dear children, I write this to you so that you will not sin. But if anybody does sin, we have an advocate with the Father – Jesus Christ, the Righteous One] the homily continues,

> If this kind of purgation will not serve them, let them never hope to be released by other men's prayers, though they should continue therein unto the world's end. He that cannot be saved by faith in Christ's blood, how shall he look to be delivered by man's intercessions? ...We must take heed that we call upon this Advocate while we have space given us in this life, lest, when we are once dead, there be no hope of salvation left unto us. For, as every man sleepeth with his own cause, so every man shall rise again with his own cause. And look, in what state he dieth, *in the same state* he shall also be judged, whether it be to salvation or damnation.[22]

5.7. The English Reformers on Purgatory

The English Reformers were unanimous in this doctrine, as may be seen from the following examples. The martyr John Frith stated in 1531, 'If thou seek another purgation, then are you injurious unto the blood of Christ; for if thou thought his blood sufficient, then wouldst thou seek no other purgatory, but give him all the thanks and all the praise of thy health and salvation, and rejoice whole in the Lord.'[23]

Thomas Cranmer, in his 1549 *Answers* to the articles of the Devon rebels, asks the question, 'If according to the catholic faith... all the faithful that die in the Lord be pardoned of all their offences by Christ, and their sins be clearly sponged and washed away by his blood; shall

---

[21] Church of England, *Sermons, or Homilies, Appointed to be Read in Churches* (London: Prayer-Book and Homily Society, 1833), p 231.
[22] Church of England, *Sermons, or Homilies*, p 232.
[23] John Frith, *The Work of John Frith*. (Ed. N. T. Wright), The Courtenay Library of Reformation Classics 7 (Appleford: Sutton Courtenay Press, 1983), p 100.

they after be cast into another strong and grievous prison of purgatory, there to be punished again for that which was pardoned before?'[24]

John Bradford in 'Confutation of Four Romish Doctrines' agrees:

> as men die, so shall they rise. Every man shall receive according to that he himself doeth in his body, while he is here alive, be it good or bad, and not according to what his executors or this chantry priest and that fraternity doth for him... they that are departed be past our prayers, either being in joy or misery; even so we having for it no word of God, whereupon faith leaneth, cannot but sin in doing it...[25]

5.8. The Articles

Article XXXI 'Of the Oblation of Christ finished upon the Cross' comments, 'the sacrifices of Masses, in the which it was commonly said, that the Priest did offer Christ for the quick and the dead, to have remission of pain or guilt, were blasphemous fables, and dangerous deceits.' The Roman Catholic teaching that Masses could be said for the dead to enable remission from time in Purgatory is seen as pure fiction and has no place in the Church of England. The Reformers clearly taught that once a death has occurred, the efforts of the living on behalf of the dead are useless. God's people gathering together to share in the Lord's Supper is for them alone, to be spiritually nourished and to remember Christ's death – it was not in any way for the benefit of those who have gone before us in the faith. This is not diminishing the importance of the sacrament – it is restoring it to its rightful place.

Article XXV 'Of the Sacraments' affirms that 'There are two sacraments ordained of Christ our Lord in the Gospel, that is to say, baptism and the Supper of the Lord.' The medieval Church held that there were *seven* sacraments. Extreme Unction (after Vatican II called 'Anointing of the Sick') at the time of death is therefore *not* accounted as a sacrament by Protestants, or necessary in any way for salvation or sanctification. Protestants did away with the ancient connection between death and the necessity of the sacraments, whereas a Roman Catholic priest would urge the dying to receive 'the Last Rites' consisting of three sacraments in the order: penance, which includes

---

[24] Thomas Cranmer, *Miscellaneous Writings and Letters of Thomas Cranmer*. John Edmund Cox (Ed.) (Cambridge: Parker Society/Cambridge University Press, 1846), pp 181-82.

[25] John Bradford, *Writings*. Ed. Aubrey Townsend (Cambridge: Parker Society/Cambridge University Press, 1848-53), Vol. 2, p 279.

absolution, extreme unction, and the *viaticum*, the last time a person takes the Eucharist, literally 'provision for the journey.' Post Reformation, death takes on a much less sacramental aspect, and thus a much less clerical aspect. Gone was the urgent rush for a priest to attend the dying, as Protestant doctrine had cut the link between priest, sacrament and death.

6. The *Book of Common Prayer* Burial Service

Cranmer knew that doctrine, liturgy and canon law all had to be reformed if the Protestant faith was to make real inroads in England. New Articles of religion were indeed promulgated, ending with the Thirty-Nine Articles drawn up in 1562 and authorised (semi-officially) in 1571 under Elizabeth.[1] Revising canon law was a much more convoluted and unsatisfactory process with the *reformatio legum* never being authorised, despite the renewed efforts of John Foxe and others decades later.[2] The *Book of Common Prayer* needs to be seen in this context of the development of Protestant formularies underpinning public life in England.

6.1. Having a set order for burials

The Church of England flatly rejected the stark Reformed order of Geneva, which was taken up wholesale in Scotland. The 1556 Geneva Book of Order states: 'The corpse is reverently brought to the grave, accompanied with the congregation, without any further ceremonies; which being buried, the minister goes to the church, if it is not far off, and makes some comfortable exhortation to the people, touching death and resurrection.'[3] But it wasn't just the more Reformed wing of the Reformation that initially had a minimum of ceremony and ritual. The first Electoral visitation commission of Saxony in 1527-8 moved to suppress minimalist nocturnal burials, which were anathema to their Catholic neighbours and also unacceptable to a developing Lutheran establishment.[4] In Strasbourg no service was held at the grave until the 1533 Synod protested, citing the burial of Old Testament patriarchs and early Christians. Four years later an Order for Burial was drawn up and

---

[1] See Gerald Bray, *The Faith we Confess: An Exposition of the Thirty-Nine Articles* (London: The Latimer Trust, 2009); Hardwick, *A History of the Articles of Religion*.

[2] See James C. Spalding, *The Reformation of the Ecclesiastical Laws of England, 1552*, Sixteenth Century Essays and Studies XIX (Kirksville, MO: Sixteenth Century Journal Publishers, 1992); John Frazier Jackson, 'The *Reformatio legum ecclesiasticarum*: Politics, Society, and Belief in mid-Tudor England' (unpublished DPhil. thesis, Oxford University, 2003); Gerald Bray (ed.), *Tudor Church Reform: The Henrician Canons of 1535 and the Reformatio Legum Ecclesiasticarum*, Church of England Record Society 8 (Woodbridge: The Boydell Press, 2000).

[3] William D. Maxwell, *The Liturgical Portions of the Genevan Service Book, used by John Knox while a minister of the English congregation of Marian exiles at Geneva, 1556-1559* (Edinburgh: The Faith Press Ltd., 1965), pp 161-64.

[4] MacCulloch, *Reformation*, p 577; Koslofsky, *The Reformation of the Dead*, pp 41-77.

used. Initial fears over superstitious usage in the past gave way to a strong pastoral incentive to in some sense honour the dead and comfort the grieving with a set service.[5]

6.2. Cranmer as editor

Cranmer's brilliance in reforming traditional material according to biblical and Protestant principles can be clearly seen in the liturgical forms he produced. The two Edwardian Books of Common Prayer of 1549 and 1552 can be, as Bryan Spinks reminds us, rightly said to be 'Cranmerian', but they are 'very far from being *ex nihilo* creations'. The archbishop did compose some fresh material, but 'he drew directly and indirectly on a wide variety of traditional and contemporary liturgical and dogmatic sources'.[6] The old Latin *Sarum Rite* is the basis of the liturgy, but with material garnered from other sources.[7] As Neil and Willoughby put it, 'While parts of the old Uses were retained, a great deal was rejected, much was added, and the whole Service entirely rearranged. It was now framed, not mainly for the benefit of the dead, but for the edification and comfort of the living.'[8] The service is clearly saturated with Scripture, as opposed to the 'unwritten verities' and unbiblical traditions of the Roman Catholic Church, which multiplied over the centuries. Perhaps the greatest concern of the Reformers was to ensure the authority in the service is provided by the Word of God.

6.3. Changes in theological emphasis

The BCP Burial Service shifts the emphasis from the Roman Catholic honouring and praying for the dead to the edification of the living. The 1549 BCP retained the prayer for the soul of the departed ('I commend thy soul to God the Father Almighty') and a celebration of Holy

---

[5] Maxwell, *Genevan Service Book*, pp 56-57.
[6] Bryan D. Spinks, 'Treasures Old and New: A Look at Some of Thomas Cranmer's Methods of Liturgical Compilation' in Paul Ayris and David Selwyn (eds.), *Thomas Cranmer: Churchman and Scholar* (Woodbridge: The Boydell Press, 1993), pp 175-88, quotation 175.
[7] For the development and sources of the BCP Burial Service, see John Henry Blunt (ed.), *The Annotated Book of Common Prayer, being an historical, ritual, and theological commentary on the devotional system of the Church of England*, rev. edn. (London: Rivingtons, 1884); Geoffrey Rowell, *The Liturgy of Christian Burial*, Alcuin Club Collections 59 (London: Alcuin Club/ SPCK, 1977); Geoffrey Cuming, *The Godly Order: Texts and Studies relating to the Book of Common Prayer* (London: Alcuin Club/ SPCK, 1983); Neil and Willoughby (eds.), *Tutorial Prayer Book*.
[8] Neil and Willoughby (eds.), *Tutorial Prayer Book*, p 470.

Communion. Bucer's comments on this earlier English Prayer Book state very clearly that both of these errors are unacceptable and should be removed.[9] The 1552 BCP indeed rejected both of these elements and considerably rearranged and altered the earlier Prayer Book. Now, the body alone is committed to the ground with the soul not addressed directly – it is the living who are the focus of the service. This has led the Catholic revisionist Eamon Duffy to state that 'the oddest feature of the 1552 rite is the disappearance of the corpse from it... at the moment of committal in 1552, the minister turns not towards the corpse, but away from it, to the living congregation around the grave.'[10] As MacCulloch argues, 'Archbishop Cranmer took great care in his much simplified final version prepared in 1552 to remove any sense that those present can do anything for the dead...his liturgy contained no sense of any continuing relationship to the corpse (or even much sense of its presence at the service).'[11]

Opponents of these Protestant ideas noted that changes to the burial service were also linked to the remodelling of the eucharistic theology. The conservative Robert Parkyn commented on the 1552 rite, 'all this was done and brought to pass only to subdue the most blessed sacrament of Christ's body and blood under form of bread and wine... no diriges or other devout prayers to be sung or said for such as was departed this transitory world'.[12] The BCP Burial Service followed the theological trajectory of the changes introduced in the Eucharist.

The old medieval fear of looming judgement is replaced by confidence ('sure and certain hope') in the resurrection of Christ, which we share. As Hague eulogises, 'Our Burial Service is indeed a service of extraordinary beauty, as is acknowledged by very many of other religious communities than our own. There runs throughout it a joyous strain of hope and happiness. Everything in it is intended to impress us with a sense of the gravity of life, the solemnity of death, and the glories and realities of the world to come.'[13]

---

[9] E.C. Whitaker, *Martin Bucer and the Book of Common Prayer*, Alcuin Club Collections 55 (Great Wakering: The Alcuin Club, 1974), pp 50-52, 126-28.

[10] Duffy, *Stripping of the Altars*, pp 473-75. Cf. Rowell, *The Liturgy of Christian Burial*, pp 84-87.

[11] MacCulloch, *Reformation*, p 577.

[12] Quoted in Diarmaid MacCulloch, *Thomas Cranmer: A Life* (New Haven; London: Yale University Press, 1996), p 509.

[13] Dyson Hague, *Through the Prayer Book: An Exposition* (London: Church Book Room Press, 1948), p 336.

6.4. *Structure of the Burial Service*

The following paragraphs detail the sources of the elements of the BCP service.

6.4.1. *Sentences (Anthem of Hope and Resurrection)*

John 11:25-26, the old Antiphon to the Benedictus in Lauds for the Dead; Job 19:25-27, the Response after the first lection in the First Nocturn for the Dead; 1 Timothy 6:7/ Job 1:21 a new addition.

6.4.2. *Psalm 39 or 90*

The Psalms in 1549 were 116, 146, 139, but these were completely omitted in 1552. In 1662 different Psalms were re-introduced (39 and 90) and their position with the Lesson was changed. The King James Version of the Bible was also preferred to that of the Great Bible of 1539. Psalm 39 is ascribed to David upon Joab's reproach for his grief for Absalom's death. It is a prayer of one who feels the vanity of all earthly things, yet finds hope in God. Because of this context, this Psalm is particularly suitable for the burial of a young person. Psalm 90 has traditionally being seen as written by Moses towards the end of the wilderness wanderings having watched many Israelites dying for their faithlessness.

6.4.3. *Bible Lesson*

1 Corinthians 15:20-58. Verses 20-23 were an alternative Epistle in the Eucharist for the Dead in the *Sarum Missal*. In 1549 it was read in the church after the Psalms either before or after the burial. In 1552 it was read by the graveside after the anthem, 'I heard a voice'. (The proposed 1928 BCP allowed 2 Corinthians 4:16–5:10.) The resurrection is explained in this wonderful reading from the Apostle Paul, emphasising the believer's vital union with Christ the 'Firstfruits'. All hostile forces have been destroyed in the overthrow of 'the last enemy' by the material, physical resurrection of Christ. The Son will resign the restored Kingdom into the Father's hands, voluntarily subjecting himself to Him.[14] As we have been endowed with a body which serves the purpose of the soul, so we shall be endowed with a body answering to the spirit. Paul's tripartite division of a human being into body, soul and spirit is

---

[14] For the Arian interpretation of this passage, see Neil and Willoughby (eds.), *Tutorial Prayer Book*, p 477. However subordination does not imply inequality.

expressly taught in 1 Thessalonians 5:23, and the contrast between soul and spirit is also brought out in Romans 8:16, and 1 Corinthians 2:11; 14:14.

6.4.4. Anthem of Lament and Supplication 'Man that is born of a woman'

First paragraph is Job 14:1-2, taken from *Sarum Breviary*, Office of the Dead. 'Man that is born of a woman' was from the fifth Lection in the *Sarum Rite*, which was the fourth Lection at Matins for the dead in the Ambrosian rite.

The ancient Latin liturgical text *Media vita* has an interesting provenance, being first translated by Luther into German, then translated into English metre in 1535 by Miles Coverdale, before Cranmer put it into prose form for both of his reformed Prayer Books, with, as MacCulloch notes, 'great success'[15]. This text is taken from the antiphon to the *Nunc Dimittis* at Compline in the *Sarum Breviary* with its versicles, as used on the third Sunday in Lent, and for fifteen days afterwards.[16]

6.4.5. Committal 'Forasmuch as it hath pleased Almighty God'

Ecclesiastes 12:7; Genesis 18:27; Genesis 3:19; Philippians 3:20-21. In 1549 these words were in the form of a commendation, addressing the corpse directly, 'I commend thy soul to God the father Almighty' etc. There was a similar, but shorter form of commendation in the *Sarum Manual*: 'I commend thy soul to God the Father, Omnipotent, earth to earth, ashes to ashes, dust to dust, in the name of the Father and of the Son, and of the Holy Spirit'. The phrase 'sure and certain hope of the resurrection to eternal life' has been a comfort to many, but has also been very controversial – see below. In 1549 'resurrection' had no article, suggesting a definiteness in regard to the dead person. Neil and Willoughby comment that, 'No one can pronounce so definitely upon another's state'.[17]

---

[15] MacCulloch, *Cranmer*, p 331; Hague, *Through the Prayer Book*, p 338. Cf. Rowell, *The Liturgy of Christian Burial*, pp 79-80. Cranmer's poetry skills did sometimes fail him. The 1662 Ordinal replaces his verse translation of the hymn *Veni Creator Spiritus* with John Cosin's accomplished version, 'Come Holy Ghost, our souls inspire'.

[16] F.E. Warren, *Prayer-Book Commentary for Teachers and Students*, 2nd. edn. (London: SPCK, 1933), p 134.

[17] Neil and Willoughby (eds.), *Tutorial Prayer Book*, p 479.

In the Committal the phrase 'our vile body' has often been misunderstood – it is not denigrating the physical body, which is part of God's good creation, but rather acknowledging that our bodies are subject to sin and death, eager to be restored in the Day of Resurrection. (The proposed 1928 BCP adds a footnote saying that 'vile body' should be understood as 'the body of our low estate'. The *Canadian Prayer Book* uses the phrase 'corruptible body', whilst *Common Worship* has 'transform our frail bodies').

6.4.6. Anthem of Assurance and Consolation 'I heard a voice from heaven'

Revelation 14:13. This was the antiphon to the *Magnificat* in Vespers for the Dead.

6.4.7. Prayers

Including The Lesser Litany, The Lord's Prayer without Doxology, and 'Almighty God, with whom do live the spirits' (Prayer for Complete Happiness of God's Church). All taken from the *Sarum Manual* and older Latin prayers e.g. a Gregorian Collect. The 1549 BCP had versicles after the Lord's Prayer, which were later dropped:

Priest	Enter not (O Lord) into judgment with thy servant.
Answer	For in thy sight no living creature shall be justified.
Priest	From the gates of hell.
Answer	Deliver their souls, O Lord.
Priest	I believe to see the goodness of the Lord.
Answer	In the land of the living.
Priest	O Lord, graciously hear my prayer.
Answer	And let my cry come unto thee.

It is no surprise that the 1552 BCP, moving in a more clearly Reformed direction, omitted these versicles as they speak of delivering souls from the gates of hell, something which only a living and active faith in Christ in the heart of the believer can achieve. To pray that souls would be delivered from hell would assume that our eternal destiny is not determined by the personal choices made in this earthly life, and that the living can influence the eternal fate of the dead, something anathema to Protestant thinking.

6.4.8. *A Prayer for the Speedy Coming of God's Kingdom and Complete Happiness of God's Church*

1549	1552	1662
O Lorde, with whom do live the spirits of them that be dead: and in whom the souls of them that be elected, after they be delivered from the burden of the flesh, be in joy and felicity: Grant unto us thy servant, that the sins which he committed in this world be not imputed unto him, but that he, escaping the gates of hell and pains of eternal darkness: may ever dwell in the region of light, with Abraham, Isaac, and Jacob, in the place where is no weeping, sorrow, nor heaviness: and when that dreadful day of the general resurrection shall come, make him to rise also with the just and righteous, and receive this body again to glory, then made pure and incorruptible, set him on the right hand of thy son Jesus Christ, among thy holy and elect, that then he may hear with them these most sweet and comfortable words: Come to me ye blessed of my father, possess the kingdom which hath been prepared for you from the beginning of the world: Grant this we beseech thee, o merciful father: through Jesus Christ our mediator and redeemer. Amen.	Almightie God, with whom do live the spirits of them that depart hence in the lord, and in whom the souls of them that be elected, after they be delivered from the burden of the flesh, be in joy and felicity: We give thee hearty thanks, for that it hath pleased thee to deliver this N. our brother out of the miseries of this sinful world: beseeching thee, that it may please thee of thy gracious goodness, shortly to accomplish the number of thy elect, and to haste thy kingdom, that we with this our brother, and all other departed in the true faith of thy holy name, may have our perfect consummation and bliss, both in body and soul, in thy eternal and everlasting glory. Amen.	Almighty God, with whom do live the spirits of them that depart hence in the Lord, and with whom the souls of the faithful, after they are delivered from the burden of the flesh, are in joy and felicity: We give thee hearty thanks, for that it hath pleased thee to deliver this our brother out of the miseries of this sinful world; beseeching thee that it may please thee, of thy gracious goodness, shortly to accomplish the number of thine elect, and to hasten thy kingdom; that we, with all those that are departed in the true faith of thy holy Name, may have our perfect consummation and bliss, both in body and soul, in thy eternal and everlasting glory; through Jesus Christ our Lord. Amen.

It is interesting to note that death is seen in all three versions as deliverance 'from the burden of the flesh', and 'the miseries of this sinful world' in 1552 and 1662. This is not denigrating this present, physical existence, but a powerful reminder to modern Christians that the best is yet to come. We are too often focussed on this present world and not the new heavens and earth the returning Christ will inaugurate. Those who have faithfully died in Christ are, contra 'soul-sleep' proponents, 'in joy and felicity' now, as they await the final consummation and a new resurrection body. It is also worthwhile noting that the theme of election is not a Protestant doctrine, but part of Catholic teaching from the earliest days of the Christian Church, based firmly on biblical attestation. God in bringing people to salvation through his Son Jesus Christ is 'accomplishing' the number of His elect.

The 1549 prayer was clearly for the dead person and this teaching was dropped in 1552 and 1662. The faithful dead are to be remembered, but the prayer is that we may share in their assured destiny. 1662 is more general and less specific about the destiny of the deceased at the service:

1552   'that we with this our brother, and all other departed in the true faith'

1662   'that we, with all those that are departed in the true faith'

The Prayer Book of 1662 concludes the phrase 'through Jesus Christ our Lord', a clear reminder that eternal salvation is not through Mary, the saints, masses for the dead, or the intercessions of the living on behalf of the departed.

6.4.9. Collect 'Merciful God, the Father of our Lord Jesus Christ'.

This prayer is a Collect, indicating that if there was a celebration of Holy Communion it is to be used in that service. It was used in this way in 1549, when the Epistle was taken from 1 Thessalonians 4:13-18 and the Gospel was from John 6:37-40.

6.4.10. The Grace.

This was introduced in 1662. The omission of the Communion Service in 1552 left the Burial Office without a suitable conclusion and the Grace provides a fitting end.

6.5. Table comparing 'The order for the Burial of the Dead' and 'The Communion Office,' 1549, with 'The Order for the Burial of the Dead,' 1662.[18]

1549	1662
The order for the Burial of the Dead	**The order for the Burial of the Dead**
At the Church stile, or going either into the Church or towards the grave.	*At the entrance of the Churchyard, either going into the Church or towards the grave.*
The Sentences	The Sentences
	In the Church
	Psalm 39 or 90
	1 Corinthians 15 Lesson
At the Grave	*At the Grave*
Opening Anthem 'Man that is born'	Opening Anthem 'Man that is born'
Committal Words	Committal Words
Closing Anthem 'I heard a voice'	Closing Anthem 'I heard a voice'
Prayer for Complete Happiness, No. 1	
1st Part 'We commend' etc.	
2nd part 'Come, ye blessed children'	
Prayer for Complete happiness, No. 2	
'Almighty God, we give thee'	
Psalms 116, 146, 139	
1 Corinthians 15 Lesson	
Lesser Litany	Lesser Litany
The Lord's Prayer	The Lord's Prayer
Suffrages	Prayer for the Complete Happiness of God's Church
Prayer for Complete happiness, No. 3	1st clause, 'Almighty God with whom'
'O Lord, with whom do live'	2nd clause, 'We give thee hearty thanks'
	Remaining clauses, 'Beseeching Thee'
	The Collect
	1st part, 'O merciful God, the Father'
	2nd part, 'Come, ye blessed'
The Celebration of the Holy Communion when there is a burial of the dead (with Epistle 1 Thessalonians 4:13-18; Gospel John 6:37-40)	The Grace

---

[18] After Neil and Willoughby *Tutorial Prayer Book*, p 472.

7. Puritan Objections to the BCP Service

The Puritans, as a renewal movement within the wider body of Protestants, were acutely aware of the spiritual training in terms of faith and knowledge that was necessary to perform their last duties on earth. To glorify God on one's death-bed was the godly man or woman's final act of witness. William Perkins described in *Salve for a Sick Man* (1597) death as 'a blessing... as it were a little wicket or door whereby we pass out of this world and enter into heaven'. The New England puritan, Increase Mather, after considering the beauty of the soul's flight to heaven, wrote 'the thought of this should make the Believer long for death'.[1] Protestant conformists, such as Lancelot Andrewes in his *A Manual of Directions for the Sick* (1648), moved away from the Puritan trait of weakening the traditional sacramental and clerical framework, and instead advocated confession of sins to a priest and the role of Holy Communion as the pledge of Christ's love to the dying Christian. This trajectory is replicated in Jeremy Taylor's *Holy Dying* (1651). The Prayer Book rubric was altered in 1662 so that the minister was urged to 'move' the sick person to make a full confession of sins.

Puritans were as much against established customs and tradition as against the rites prescribed in the Prayer Book. Some stipulated that they be buried 'without popish pomp, vain compliments and ringing'. Others insisted that burial was not the prerogative of the minister alone and all godly Christians should see it as their duty. Many simply could not accept that the service could be used for those whose reputation strongly suggested that they were not to be numbered among the godly. In Philip Henry's Shropshire parish when 'an old man of evil name' was buried according to the *Book of Common Prayer* 'it caused great offence'. Henry attended a funeral of an adversary for the sermon, 'but went forth when Common Prayer was to be read at the grace, some expressions in the prayers I cannot approve, especially upon some occasions and particularly this'.[2] Puritans were often ambivalent about funeral sermons. Although they were cautious of flattery and civil orations replacing the true preaching of God's Word, the godly came to expect a sermon as part of the burial customs.

---

[1] Quoted in Stannard, *Puritan way of Death*.
[2] Quoted in John Spurr, *English Puritanism, 1603-1689* (Basingstoke: Macmillan, 1998), p 33.

In the Puritan grievances catalogued in the 1593 'Second Part of a Register' an anonymous correspondent complains that 'the pastor's office being only the ministry of the word and sacraments... is further with us surcharged with the burial of the dead, and special service for it'. Another asserts that 'Burial of the dead pertains no more to the minister than to the rest of the congregation'. When questioned about his nonconformity in this regard, John Udall stated 'that in the primitive church the dead were buried by their friends, and burial was not a function of the minister until the time of popery.'[3] In 1584 a Puritan was interrogated over his subscription to the archbishop's articles. The anonymous puritan questions, 'Whether it be not absurd, whensoever the minister burieth Protestant, Papist, or Atheist, Heretic, Usurer, or Whoremonger, good or bad, to say that he is his brother, as the book appointeth, and that he committeth him to the ground... in sure and certain hope of resurrection to eternal life?' Clearly, an indiscriminate use of liturgy which assumes the conversion of the deceased was problematic to many with Puritan leanings.[4]

7.1. The Admonition Controversy (1572-77)

In 1572 two young Puritans, John Field and Thomas Willcox, wrote an incendiary pamphlet called 'An Admonition to Parliament' which spelt out in no uncertain terms the faults of the Prayer Book and its services. The 'Admonition' has this to say about the burial service:

> They appoint a prescript kind of service to bury the dead: And that which is the duty of every Christian, they tie alone to the minister, whereby prayer for the dead is maintained, and partly gathered out of some of the prayers, where they pray that we with this our brother, and all other departed in the true faith of thy holy name, may have our perfect consummation and bliss, both in body and soul. We say nothing of the threefold peal because that it is rather licensed by injunction, then commanded in their book, nor of their strange mourning by changing their garments, which if it be not

---

[3] Albert Peel (ed.), *The Seconde Parte of a Register: Being a Calendar of Manuscripts under that Title intended for Publication by the Puritans about 1593, and now in Dr. Williams's Library, London* (Cambridge: Cambridge University Press, 1915), Vol. 1, pp 132, 259; Vol. 2, p 45.

[4] Albert Peel (ed.), *The Seconde Parte of a Register*, Vol. 1, p 201. 'It is impossible to commit notorious sinners to the grave in sure and certain hope of resurrection to everlasting life.' Vol. 1, p 242. Others felt the words "in sure and certain hope etc.' tend to superstition'. Vol. 2, p 204.

hypocritical, yet it is superstitious and heathenish, because it is used only of custom, nor of burial sermons, which are put in place of trentals,[5] where out spring many abuses, and therefore in the best reformed churches, are removed. As for the superstitions used both in Country and City, for the place of burial, which way they must lie, how they must be fetched to church, the minister meeting them at church stile with surplice, with a company of greedy clerks, that a cross white or black, must be set upon the dead corpse, that bread must be given to the poor, and offerings in burial time used, and cakes sent abroad to friends, because these are rather used of custom and superstition, then by the authority of the book. Small commandment will serve for the accomplishing of such things. But great charge will hardly bring the least good thing to pass, and therefore all is let alone, and the people as blind and as ignorant as ever they were. God be merciful unto us.[6]

The Admonition serves as a useful focal point of Puritan grievances – many disliked prescript services instead of extempore prayers, and played down the role of ordained, sacrament-dispensing clergy, seeing ministry at the time of death as the duty of all believers. Some saw that 'prayer for the dead is maintained', yet this is hard to observe in the Elizabethan Prayer Book. Puritans disliked many of the popish trappings that still accompanied burials, though recognising these were not authorized or encouraged by the Prayer Book. The authors of the Admonition do make the point that a Protestant national liturgy does not stop many of the people being as spiritually blind as before the Reformation, but in time, most of these traditional customs surrounding death and burial did die out.

7.2. The Savoy Conference (1661)

At the Restoration the Puritan party was declining and concessions from the bishops were minimal. There was a shared Protestant consensus between bishop and Puritan, and therefore, as Buchanan

---

[5] A trental is a Roman Catholic office and mass for the dead on the 30th day after death or burial. From the Latin *'triginta'*, thirty.
[6] W. H. Frere and C. E. Douglas (eds.), *Puritan Manifestoes: A Study of the Origin of the Puritan Revolt* (London: S.P.C.K. for Church Historical Society, 1907), p 28.

notes, 'they did not encounter a need to discuss petitions for the dead'.[7] 'The General Exceptions' from the Puritan party at the conference focus on the three traditional Puritan complaints of wearing the surplice, signing with the cross at baptism, and kneeling at Communion. 'The Particular Exceptions' include 'Of the Order for the Burial of the Dead', where the Puritans state, 'We desire it may be expressed in a Rubric, that the Prayers and Exhortations here used are not for the benefit of the Dead, but only for the Instruction and Comfort of the Living.' They also wanted to use their own discretion about particular circumstances of location to avoid 'those Inconveniences which many times both Ministers and People are exposed unto by standing in the open Air'.[8] The bishops sarcastically respond, 'the desire that all may be said in the Church, being not pretended to be for the ease of tender consciences, but of tender heads, may be helped by a Cap, better than a Rubric'. The 1552 service was all in the churchyard, but the 1662 BCP made much more provision for holding the service in the church. Having a service all in the churchyard could have been for reasons of health (not having diseased corpses in the enclosed church), or to get away from the church building being somehow a holy space suitable for burials. It is well known that many wanted to be buried in the church as near as possible to the altar for supposed spiritual benefit.

The Puritans baulked at the by now notorious phrase 'sure and certain hope of Resurrection to eternal life', and the use of 'dear Brother' and 'our brother' to refer to all those who were to be buried: 'These words cannot in Truth be said of Persons living and dying in open and notorious sins... These words cannot be used with respect to those Persons who have not by their actual Repentance given any ground for the hope of their Blessed Estate'.[9] This was a familiar tension in a national liturgy: how to produce Christian liturgy for all, but retaining a belief that it only applies to some. The bishops' response is worth quoting in full as an important liturgical principle:

---

[7] Colin Buchanan, *The Savoy Conference Revisited*, Joint Liturgical Studies 54 (Cambridge: The Alcuin Club/ The Group for Renewal of Worship, 2002), p 7. 'Puritan' here refers to Presbyterians, as the Independents would have nothing to do with a set liturgy and conference with the bishops. For documents of the conference, see Edward Cardwell, *A History of Conferences and Other Proceedings Connected with the Revision of the Book of Common Prayer; from the year 1558 to the Year 1690* 3rd. edn. (Oxford: Oxford University Press, 1849).

[8] Buchanan, *The Savoy Conference Revisited*, p 72.

[9] Buchanan, *The Savoy Conference Revisited*, p 74; Cardwell, *A History of Conferences*, p 333.

We see not why these words may not be said of any person, who we dare not say is damned; and it were a breach of Charity to say so, even of those whose repentance we do not see: For whether they do not inwardly, and heartily repent, even at the last act, who knows? And that God will not even then pardon them upon such repentance, who dares say? It is better to be Charitable, and hope the best, than rashly to condemn.[10]

Yet, despite the above 'Answer' to Puritan scruples, the bishops at the conference did make a concession with the omission of 'sure and certain', i.e. not saying categorically that the dead person will have eternal life. This concession did not, however, find its way into the 1662 BCP. A new rubric however forbids the use of the burial service for 'any that die unbaptized, or excommunicate, or have laid violent hands upon themselves.' In the 1662 BCP 'hope of resurrection' has become 'hope of *the* resurrection', 'a general affirmation, less related to the particular dead person.'[11]

Richard Baxter, one of the Presbyterian Puritans attending the conference, set down in his 'Savoy Liturgy' what his understanding of Christian burial was. He makes little dispute about the service order, 'Let no Christians uncharitably judge one another about these things', as the main principle is that 'the burial of Christians be solemnly and decently performed.' Baxter is adamant that the minister is to 'gravely discourse of man's mortality', the actual location of the discourse, whether at grave, reading-place, or pulpit, is not the issue. The minister is to 'instruct and exhort the people concerning death, and the life to come, and their necessary preparation; seeing the spectacle of mortality, and the season of mourning, do tend to prepare men for a sober, considerate entertainment of such instructions'. Funeral sermons were originally frowned upon by some Puritans, such as the authors of 'the Admonition' (above), but towards the end of the 17th Century they had become important vehicles for godly exhortation and evangelism. Again, because of the vagaries of British weather, Baxter suggests that, 'Whenever the rain, snow, or coldness of the season make it unhealthful to the minister or people to stand out of doors, at least let the reading, exhortation and prayers, be used within the church'.[12]

---

[10] Buchannan 'The Savoy Conference Revisited', p 75.
[11] Buchanan, *The Savoy Conference Revisited*, p 78.
[12] Rowell, *The Liturgy of Christian Burial*, pp 92-93.

For the evangelical using the BCP Burial Service some of these Puritan objections and answers are still pertinent. If the service suggests that everyone is to be saved and has a 'sure and certain hope of Resurrection to Eternal Life', that is a dangerous universalism to be avoided. If a minister is conducting a funeral of an unknown parishioner, as is often the case, then definitive pronouncements as to their eternal destiny are to be avoided. The limits of being charitable in liturgy are not always clear. Death-bed conversions as imagined by the bishops are certainly possible, but to presume upon them is another thing entirely. Perhaps it is the link between the liturgy and the sermon that is crucial in this regard – the sermon needs to explain the truths of the biblical Gospel, reinforcing the liturgy where it is helpful and clear, and explaining the true interpretation of the BCP where it is not. It is also to be remembered that parish clergy are obligated to provide a funeral service for anyone who lives in their parish.

7.3. *Later Evangelicals and the BCP Burial Service*

Later Evangelicals in the Church of England wanted to defend their cause against both non-conformity and other Anglicans. Charles Simeon was part of a long line of evangelicals who, *contra* many Puritans before them, wished to align themselves whole-heartedly with the Prayer Book and the Articles, as that was also demonstrably the faith of the New Testament. Simeon's influential 1812 work *The Excellency of the Liturgy* defends both a set form of prayers and the more controversial phrases of the Prayer Book, including 'sure and certain hope of the resurrection to eternal life' in the Burial Service. Simeon admits that the Prayer Book, being 'a human composition', is not perfect and notes that this controversial phrase 'might be altered for the better' and 'might admit of some improvement'. As Andrew Atherstone notes,

> objections to these parts of the *Book of Common Prayer* were a contributory factor in the flurry of evangelical secessions from the Church of England in the early nineteenth century, both in the mid-1810s in the south-west of England (the so-called 'Western Schism') and again at Oxford in the early 1830s. For example, Charles Brenton (curate of Stadhampton near Oxford) refused in 1831 to read the Burial Service over a notorious drunkard who had been the parish-clerk for 40 years. He preached a fiery sermon defending his actions, proclaiming that it was absurd, impious, wicked, blasphemous and hypocritical to use the Prayer Book funeral liturgy

for 'baptized infidels', and announced to the congregation his intention to resign his ministry and leave the Church.[13]

Simeon noted that Bible passages such as Galatians 3:27 and 1 Peter 3:21 would also make uncomfortable reading for those who had scruples about the Church of England's official liturgy. The Bible should not be moulded into any partisan theological system – a certain latitude of interpretation was necessary. Simeon's third sermon in *The Excellency of the Liturgy* states,

> From our very birth even to the grave, our Church omits nothing that can tend to the edification of its members... even after death, when she can no more benefit the deceased, the Church labours to promote the benefit of her surviving members, by a service the most solemn and impressive that ever was formed.[14]

---

[13] Andrew Atherstone, *Charles Simeon on the Excellency of the Liturgy*, Joint Liturgical Studies 72 (Norwich: Alcuin Club/ The Group for Renewal of Worship, 2011), p 27.

[14] Atherstone, *Charles Simeon on the Excellency of the Liturgy*, pp 34-35, 40.

8. Anglican Liturgy after the BCP

8.1. The 1928 Prayer Book

Although favoured by many in the Church of England, Parliament refused to authorise the deposited 1928 BCP, particularly because it allowed for the first time since the Reformation ritualistic elements such as the reserved sacrament and eucharistic vestments. As we have already seen, it also re-introduced to the Calendar 'The Collect for the Commemoration of All Souls' (2 Nov), a sure sign that it was the Anglo-Catholic party that was driving the proposed changes to the national liturgy. As the Church of England website informs us, 'In 1966 most of the 1928 services were legally authorized for use in public worship – some in amended form – as the First Series of Alternative Services.'[1] The 'Series One' Burial Services, containing the 1928 material in a revised order, are still part of the Church of England's authorized liturgy. The most important alterations are: The long lesson from 1 Corinthians 15 is now optional (2 Corinthians 4:16–5:10; Revelation 7:9-17 or 21:1-7 are provided), a greater choice is given of psalms (Psalms 23 and 130 are alternatives), and a prayer for consecration of the grave is provided, in case the cemetery is not consecrated. A service for the burial of a baptised child is also given.

After the appointed Psalms the *Gloria Patri* may be substituted by 'rest eternal grant unto them, O Lord: and let light perpetual shine upon them' – another indication of the direction that the 1928 Prayer Book was moving in. The familiar words of committal are now given an alternative prayer:

---

[1] https://www.churchofengland.org/prayer-worship/worship/texts/1928.aspx. Accessed 11th July 2015.

1662 BCP

Forasmuch as it hath pleased Almighty God of his great mercy to take unto himself the soul of our dear brother here departed: we therefore commit his body to the ground; earth to earth, ashes to ashes, dust to dust; in sure and certain hope of the Resurrection to eternal life, through our Lord Jesus Christ; who shall change our vile body, that it may be like unto his glorious body, according to the mighty working, whereby he is able to subdue all things to himself.

1928 Proposal

We commend unto thy hands of mercy, most merciful Father, the soul of this our *brother* departed, and we commit *his* body to the ground, earth to earth, ashes to ashes, dust to dust ; and we beseech thine infinite goodness to give us grace to live in thy fear and love and to die in thy favour, that when the judgement shall come which thou hast committed to thy well-beloved Son, both this our *brother* and we may be found acceptable in thy sight. Grant this, O merciful Father, for the sake of Jesus Christ, our only Saviour, Mediator, and Advocate. *Amen.*

Commendation again sounds like the salvation of a person may be influenced by the prayers and efforts of the living. Praying that the dead may be 'found acceptable' in God's sight seems to reckon the issue of eternal salvation not to the individual's decision during their life, but to the efficacy of prayers once they are dead.

Another alternative, the addition of the slightly modified versicles of 1549 (based on Psalms 143:2; 86:13; 27:13; 102:1) reflects the same movement in the pre-Reformation direction of interceding for the dead:

1549 BCP

Priest Enter not (O Lord) into judgment with thy servant.
Answer For in thy sight no living creature shall be justified.
Priest From the gates of hell.
Answer Deliver their souls, O Lord.
Priest I believe to see the goodness of the Lord.
Answer In the land of the living.
Priest O Lord, graciously hear my prayer.
Answer And let my cry come unto thee.

1928 Proposal

The following Versicles and Responses may then be said by the Minister and people.
Minister Enter not into judgement with thy servant, O Lord
Answer For in thy sight shall no man living be justified.
Minister Grant unto him eternal rest;
Answer And let perpetual light shine upon him.
Minister We believe verily to see the goodness of the Lord
Answer In the land of the living.
Minister O Lord, hear our prayer;
Answer And let our cry come unto thee.

Before the final blessing of the Grace (2 Corinthians 13: 13), three new prayers are included, the first of which is a clear move in the direction of prayer for the dead. If we pray that God would continue to 'work in them' after death, a sense of progression after death is envisaged, which diminishes the saving and purging work of Christ:

> FATHER of all, we pray to thee for those whom we love, but see no longer. Grant them thy peace; let light perpetual shine upon them; and in thy loving wisdom and almighty power work in them the good purpose of thy perfect will; through Jesus Christ our Lord. Amen.

Provision is made for hymns and for this order being used at a cremation. A more controversial provision is also made for 'a special celebration of the Holy Communion on the day of the burial', which was a feature of the 1549 BCP consciously omitted in the Reformation era Prayer Books, as it brought back the unbiblical and unhelpful notion of saying Mass for the souls of the dead. The readings for Holy Communion are given as 1 Thessalonians 4:13-18 (as in 1549) or 2 Corinthians 4:16–5:4 for the Epistle, and John 6:37-41 (again, as 1549) or John 5:24-29. At the end of the 1928 proposal we have the following option:

> *If the ground be not consecrated, the Priest on coming to the grave may say the prayer following.*
>
> O GOD, the Father of our Lord Jesus Christ, vouchsafe, we beseech thee, to bless this grave to be the peaceful resting-place of the body of thy servant; through the same thy blessed Son, who is the resurrection and the life, and who liveth and reigneth with thee and the Holy Ghost; one God, world without end. Amen.

We have mentioned above that Protestantism sought to demystify space and ground, removing cause of dangerous superstitious beliefs and practices that built up around death and burial in the medieval period. The blessing of inanimate objects, such as a grave or the water at a baptism has always been controversial.

8.2. The Alternative Service Book (1980)

The *ASB* follows the more modern liturgical trend of offering many variations and alternatives and thus moving away from the idea of 'common prayer' i.e. a form of service invariably used in every Church of England church. The rubric denying the service to suicides and the unbaptised was simply omitted. The *ASB* also takes into consideration the modern realities of cremation, of having the option of the committal preceding the service etc. There are a large range of Opening Sentences, Readings (including some from the Apocrypha), and Psalms to choose from. A new prayer is offered with a strong confessional tone to use our time correctly here on earth, following the example of Christ:

> Grant us, Lord, the wisdom and the grace to use aright the time that is left to us here on earth. Lead us to repent of our sins, the evil we have done and the good we have not done; and strengthen us to follow the steps of your Son, in the way that leads to the fullness of eternal life; through Jesus Christ our Lord. Amen.

There follows a commendation, and then this prayer:

> May God in his infinite love and mercy bring the whole Church, living and departed in the Lord Jesus, to a joyful resurrection and the fulfilment of his eternal kingdom. Amen.

This emphasis on the Communion of Saints, the Church militant and triumphant, living and departed, is an important theological emphasis which we can often lose, but the danger is that we think that one can influence the other through our prayers. Praying for the faithful 'departed in the Lord' will be misleading and open to misinterpretation. The *ASB* service concludes with the traditional 'Man born of a woman' prayer' and a modified and shortened committal:

1662 BCP Committal

Forasmuch as it hath pleased Almighty God of his great mercy to take unto himself the soul of our dear brother here departed: we therefore commit his body to the ground; earth to earth, ashes to ashes, dust to dust; in sure and certain hope of the Resurrection to eternal life, through our Lord Jesus Christ; who shall change our vile body, that it may be like unto his glorious body, according to the mighty working, whereby he is able to subdue all things to himself.

1980 ASB Committal

We have entrusted our brother N to God's merciful keeping, and we now commit his body to the ground (or to be cremated): [earth to earth, ashes to ashes, dust to dust;] in sure and certain hope of the resurrection to eternal life through our Lord Jesus Christ, who died, was buried, and rose again for us. To him be glory for ever and ever.

What we lose from the *BCP* is the sense of God's sovereignty in ordering our life and death – it pleased God to take the soul of the departed and God is able to subdue all things to himself. Perhaps it was considered unfit for modern people to acknowledge that a death, in any sense, could be pleasing to God and was part of his overall purposes. This sense of God being in absolute control of our earthly and eternal existence was a very powerful and pervasive feature of much Puritan literature on death and dying. The time of our death is in God's control and care. The *ASB* also omits the transformation of our vile body to be like Christ's glorious body, thus losing out on the richness of the theological truth of a renewed resurrection body, following on from Christ's resurrected body being the first-fruits of a redeemed and renewed humanity. The service ends with verses from Psalm 16:11 and Jude 24, 25.

The *ASB* provides a separate 'The Funeral of a Child' with different readings (Mark 10: 13-16; Ephesians 3:14-19); 'Prayers after the Birth of a still-born Child or the Death of a newly-born Child'; 'A Form which may be used at the Interment of the Ashes', 'A Service which may be used before a Funeral' and provision for 'The Funeral Service with Holy Communion'.

The service which 'may be used before a funeral' brings back the pre-Reformation practice of a vigil held over the corpse before the actual funeral service. It is not explained why this is pastorally necessary, or desirable. Readings, Psalms, and prayers are appointed for the occasion. The rubric at the end adds, 'Alternatively, this service may be said in the home before the body is taken to the church'. Again, this takes away from the public act of worship and seems to focus on the service being for the dead rather than the living, which is the constant *BCP* emphasis.

8.3. Common Worship (2000)

It seems that when we come to *Common Worship* that Church of England worship has moved very far from the theological principles imbedded in the *Book of Common Prayer*. The 'official' handbook to go with the new services comments that the new liturgy is for those 'who found the seventeenth-century language and imagery of the Prayer Book unhelpful'.[2] The Introduction to this handbook, from a member of the

---

[2] R. Anne Horton, *Using Common Worship: Funerals. A Practical Guide to the new Services.* (London: Church House Publishing, 2000), p xi.

Liturgical Commission, states clearly their approach 'by taking the basic structure, for the first time since the Reformation in the Church of England, not the Office but the Eucharist'. There is an explicit attempt to 'open the door to looking again at Funerals as a continuum of rites, a series of prayers and services'.[3] It is the view of the handbook that the Reformers, desperate to get rid of the problems associated with prayer for the dead, purgatory and other corrupt medieval practices, threw the baby out with the bath water. A single service is now replaced with 'staged rites', a breaking up of the rite into different stages, both before and after the central event of the burial. The key idea is that of movement, between place of death, place of worship, and place of burial. Busy parish ministers may wonder how they can possibly provide the numerous extra stages envisaged in *Common Worship*. Most families who come to the Church for a funeral will not be aware or even want the extra elements of prayer at the time of death, at home after the funeral etc.

Gone, therefore, is the streamlined, Reformed simplicity of 'The Order for the Burial of the Dead' in the Prayer Book, to be replaced by a plethora of services, variations and loose liturgical frameworks, which only professional clergy can ever hope to understand:

Ministry at the Time of Death

Before the Funeral

At Home before the Funeral
For those unable to be Present at the Funeral
Receiving the Coffin at Church before the Funeral
A Funeral Vigil
On the Morning of the Funeral

The Funeral

The Outline Order for Funerals
The Funeral Service

---

[3] Horton, *Using Common Worship*, pp 6, 11. The central, crisis event is labelled 'liminal' (LAT. *limen*, 'threshold'). This is the actual burial, the events before are 'pre-liminary' and the events after, 'post-liminal'. Therefore in this staged rites thinking, ministry at time of death, prayers at home before the funeral, receiving of the body into church etc. are all pre-liminal; the burial itself liminal; prayers said on returning home, memorial services, burial of ashes etc. are post-liminal. This is a return to medieval thinking, which the Reformers sought to move away from, because of all the superstitious practices which came to be associated with stages of death and burial.

The Funeral Service within a Celebration of Holy Communion
Supplementary Tests, including The Blessing of a Grave
The Outline Order for the Funeral of a Child
The Outline Order for the Funeral of a Child within a celebration of Holy Communion
Resources for the Funeral of a Child

After the Funeral

At Home after the Funeral
The Burial of Ashes
An Outline Order for a Memorial Service
An Outline Order for a Memorial Service within a Celebration of Holy Communion

Resources

Prayers for Use with the Dying and at Funeral and Memorial Services
Bible Readings and Psalms for Use at Funeral and Memorial Services
Canticles for Use at Funeral and Memorial Services

The official handbook acknowledges that in *Common Worship* 'we have moved a long way from the world of The *Book of Common Prayer*... there are so many different texts' compared to previous provision. 'A further look at the details of the provision also indicates a distinct move in emphasis. No longer are we concerned solely with the reverent disposal of a body in the context of Christian faith and worship, important though that is. We are now honouring the life and relationships of the dead person and the pastoral care of living people – sick people, dying people, bereaved people.'[4] (It is important to remember that the *Book of Common Prayer* does provide pastoral care and liturgical provision in its services 'The Communion of the Sick' and 'Order for the Visitation of the Sick' and these should be perhaps better known and practiced.)

Common Worship, as a movement of liturgical revision since the Prayer Book, sought to 'lessen the almost harsh austerity of the 1662 service', when death often came 'swiftly and suddenly'.[5] *Common Worship* attempted to rectify the *ASB*'s perceived over-emphasis on resurrection joy against the natural human emotions of grief, confusion and doubt. *Common Worship* also acknowledges doctrinal variation within the Church of England:

---

[4] Horton, *Using Common Worship*, pp 20, 33.
[5] Horton, *Using Common Worship*, p 33.

> The varied understandings in the Church of England over specific prayer for the departed have been carefully addressed. The prayers in the basic Funeral service are acceptable to all. Those who would wish to make specific prayer for the departed will find that some of the optional prayers for use with those who are dying can be adapted for this alternative context.[6]

This is a clear departure from Articles XXII and XXXI, which set down the principle that the living cannot influence the eternal salvation and resting place of the dead. There is the added confusion that *Common Worship* provides plenty of commended texts as well as authorised texts; the former are 'optional additional resources', which although commended by the House of Bishops, 'they have not had to undergo the full synodical authorisation treatment'. The distinction between authorised and commended prayers within the covers of the same book will clearly be lost over time and in practice and represents a way of widening the doctrinal basis of the Church of England by stealth. David Phillips comments that the prayer in the Funeral Service 'Bring all who rest in Christ into the fullness of your kingdom where sins have been forgiven and death is no more', 'seems to imply that those who currently rest in Christ have not yet been forgiven. Whereas, if we are in Christ now, we are forgiven, because we are justified by faith. Such a confused prayer can be taken to imply the existence of purgatory.'[7] Any suggestion of spiritual progress or development *post mortem* can open the door to both intercession for the dead and the idea of further cleansing from sin being necessary in an intermediate state.

There is further confusion when an 'outline order' for a funeral service is provided giving the necessary content, or 'authorised framework' (gathering, readings and sermon, prayers, commendation and farewell, committal, dismissal), but not stipulating which actual texts are to be used. Some may see this as a modern, flexible approach to varying pastoral needs in the parish, but this is also a departure from the whole Anglican principle of common prayer, when a Church of England funeral service would be instantly recognisable as such, and not dependent on location, or the minister conducting the service. It also diminishes the role of liturgy as a vehicle for doctrinal and biblical teaching.

---

[6] Horton, *Using Common Worship*, p 35.
[7] Phillips, 'What should we pray? Prayer for the dead in Anglican liturgy'.

8.4. The Funeral Service

A summary structure of the service, with optional elements in square brackets:

The Gathering
[Sentences]
Introduction
[Prayer]
[Prayers of Penitence]
The Collect
Readings and Sermon
Prayers
Commendation and Farewell
The Committal
The Dismissal

Common Worship has introduced several new elements into the Funeral Service – the possibility of a pall (signifying the baptismal status of the deceased) being placed over the coffin, the sprinkling of the coffin with water, and a candle accompanying the coffin. The words of Introduction are new and explain the purpose of a funeral – remembering, giving thanks, commending, committing and comforting. The deceased is explicitly referred to as 'brother/sister *N*', something which, as we have seen, the Puritans of a previous generation baulked at. Then follows two optional prayers, 'the first prayer is possibly the more appropriate one for a largely Christian congregation, the second for a more mixed gathering, possibly at a crematorium'.[8]

A tribute is mentioned at this point to acknowledge the deceased person's life and achievements. It is the first official liturgical mention of a practice with a very long heritage. An official note (Pastoral Services, Note 4, p 291) suggests that 'if the occasion demands it may be woven into the sermon', but it is probably more helpful to separate the tribute from the sermon, so the first part of the service reflects upon the deceased and the second part concentrates on God's Word and the proclamation of Christian hope. The congregation then understand and experience that the last word on a person is God's Word, a vital theological insight.

---

[8] Horton, *Using Common Worship: Funerals. A Practical Guide to the new Services*, p 43.

Prayers of Penitence follow as an option and it is helpful to realise the extent of human frailty and sin which finds a very natural expression in confession and repentance.

The Collect is an essential text focussing on the need for a strengthening of faith that all who have died in the love of Christ will share in his resurrection. Alternative collects are available in the resources section.

In the readings and sermon section a psalm or hymn must be included together with at least a New Testament reading and a sermon. Psalm 23 is included in the service for easy use.

Prayers are suggested in the sequence: thanksgiving for life of the departed, for those who mourn, penitence (if not already used), readiness to live in the light of eternity. The handbook states that there are 'no prayers for the departed in the authorized Funeral material', but alternative prayers of entrusting and commending may be appropriate for those whose custom it is to pray for the dead.

> The agreed *Common Worship* policy is that the authorized printed Funeral texts should only contain words and prayers that everyone should feel able to use. There is, however, freedom within the rubrics for ministers to choose and use the prayers they consider the most appropriate.'[9]

The official handbook for *Common Worship* funerals readily acknowledges the fact of a 'spectrum of sincerely held theological positions' and the new provisions had to be acceptable to all. Michael Perham and Christopher Cocksworth are held up as representative examples of the 'more catholic than reformed' and 'more reformed than catholic' parties respectively. The compromise position is that 'the 'standard service' fulfils the doctrinal requirements of the 'more reformed' Anglican, while the alternative prayers and supplementary texts include some additional material, the careful use of which might supply the further doctrinal dimension hoped for by 'more catholic' Anglicans'.[10]

The Commendation is a prayer that entrusts the deceased person to God's merciful keeping and it provides a locus for the end of a church service if, as is often the case, a smaller committal happens afterwards

---

[9] Horton, *Using Common Worship*, p 46.
[10] Horton, *Using Common Worship*, p 124.

elsewhere. A variety of alternatives are provided, including for infants and children.

1662 *BCP* Committal	1980 *ASB* Committal	2000 *CW* Committal
Forasmuch as it hath pleased Almighty God of his great mercy to take unto himself the soul of our dear brother here departed: we therefore commit his body to the ground; earth to earth, ashes to ashes, dust to dust; in sure and certain hope of the Resurrection to eternal life, through our Lord Jesus Christ; who shall change our vile body, that it may be like unto his glorious body, according to the mighty working, whereby he is able to subdue all things to himself.	We have entrusted our brother N to God's merciful keeping, and we now commit his body to the ground (or to be cremated): [earth to earth, ashes to ashes, dust to dust;] in sure and certain hope of the resurrection to eternal life through our Lord Jesus Christ, who died, was buried, and rose again for us. To him be glory for ever and ever.	We have entrusted our brother/sister N to God's mercy, and we now commit his/her body to the ground: earth to earth, ashes to ashes, dust to dust: in sure and certain hope of the resurrection to eternal life through our Lord Jesus Christ, who will transform our frail bodies that they may be conformed to his glorious body, who died, was buried, and rose again for us. To him be glory for ever. *All:* Amen.

The texts of the committal in *Common Worship* are very similar to the *ASB* and verses from Psalm 103 are retained in two sets, the latter being closer to the *BCP*. Three committal prayers are provided – at the burial of the body, at a cremation, and when ashes are buried in a churchyard or cemetery at some later date. The last committal variation sees the cremation as a preparation for burial. The dismissal is given an important ending role with several different variations, including the *Nunc Dimittis* and a blessing, allowed. The Lord's Prayer is said, if not used already.

8.5. *Summary of the Common Worship funeral services*

It is not to be denied that *Common Worship* gives a huge variety of provisions for pastoral care and instruction during the time of death and burial. The resource sections do contain useful prayers in the case of funerals for suicides, children etc. There is a notable emphasis on celebrating resurrection hope, acknowledging the achievements of a God-given life, and preparation for eternal life. But for those who hold to the doctrines espoused in the Prayer Book, Articles and Ordinal, there are serious concerns.

Firstly, the guiding principles of movement, being on a journey and 'staged rites' diminishes the centrality of a single burial service with a simple, uncluttered arrangement.

Secondly, such a variety of provision and use of frameworks takes away from the idea of a national, common worship.

Thirdly, *Common Worship* allows doctrine contrary to the Anglican formularies to be tolerated, if not positively encouraged.

9. The Modern British Funeral

9.1. Britain Today

The Anglican Evangelical minister today is living in a very different context from that of the 17th Century, and it would be wrong to suggest the complete Prayer Book Burial Service is the best option in every situation. The UK is now a pluralist, multicultural society, with many people of different faiths, or no faith.[1] How then to apply the biblical, Protestant principles of the *BCP* to our present situation?

Around half a million funerals are conducted in the UK each year and from a purely business point of view the 'funeral market' is worth more than £1 billion annually. Most of the 4,000 UK funeral directors prefer cremations over burials for reasons of cost and time.[2] It is simply a fact that the Christian minister has to interact positively and engage with undertakers, who are part of an industry which represents the professionalization of death and funerals in much of Western culture. According to the Church of England's latest annual statistics, 'Church of England Clergy and lay ministers conducted 162,526 funerals in 2011... On these figures the Church of England conducted an average of over 3,000 funerals every week in 2011 – over 400 every day.'[3] In 2011 there were 455,100 deaths in England, of these 162,526 Church of England funerals resulted i.e. just 36% of the total. Of these funerals 86,590 were held in churches, only 53% of the total. The rest were held in crematoria and cemetery chapels. Church of England funerals in churches therefore represent only 19% of all deaths in England, less than one on five.

---

[1] In the 2011 Census, Christianity was the largest religion, with 33.2 million people (59.3 per cent of the population). The second largest religious group were Muslims with 2.7 million people (4.8 per cent of the population). 14.1 million people, around a quarter of the population in England and Wales, reported they have no religion in 2011. The religion question was the only voluntary question on the 2011 census and 7.2 per cent of people did not answer the question. Between 2001 and 2011 there has been a decrease in people who identify as Christian (from 71.7 per cent to 59.3 per cent) and an increase in those reporting no religion (from 14.8 per cent to 25.1 per cent).' Http://www.ons.gov.uk/ons/rel/census/2011-census/key-statistics-for-local-authorities-in-england-and-wales/rpt-religion.html. Accessed 13 October 2015.

[2] See Appendix 1 for the choice of cremation as opposed to burial.

[3] http://www.churchofengland.org/media-centre/news/2013/05/church-annual-statistics-for-2011.aspx. Accessed 16 June 2014. The Church of England analysis relies on the data supplied from the Office of National Statistics for deaths per year.

9.2. *Practical Arrangements*

A minister having a 25-30 minute 'slot at the crem' is a reality that many people are familiar with, whether they be undertakers, the bereaved family, ministers, or those attending a service. If the decision is made to use the *BCP* burial rite, the service will need to be tailored for that occasion. The minister may also be asked to separate the burial service from the committal, happening either before or after the main service of thanksgiving and remembrance. In terms of pastoral care, the minister will usually meet with the family before the service to make the necessary arrangements and to consider hymns, readings etc. Trying to organise a funeral without a face-to-face meeting with the family is very difficult, but in some instances unavoidable. Ministers will have to be welcoming yet firm in allowing some readings and musical items and not others.[4] A truly Gospel focussed funeral will have to be sensitive to the wishes of the family, patient in explaining what the priorities are, and firm in ruling out unhelpful content. As well as inappropriate music, clergy are used to receiving odd requests, for example, releasing of doves at the graveside, odd-shaped coffins, milk floats as a hearse and so on. Having a pre-prepared guide to funerals with examples of suitable readings and music may be helpful to give to non-church families organising a funeral – often a bewildering and stressful time for many. Attending the reception or hospitality after the service should be a priority, as it often provides invaluable opportunities for pastoral care and evangelism. In the case of cremation there may be the interment of ashes in a churchyard or memorial garden at some later point. Again, this can be a fruitful Gospel opportunity when carefully thought and prayed through.

The vast majority of Church of England funerals, whether in a church or crematorium, will be carried out using the liturgy in the *Common Worship* 'Pastoral Services' book. Only in a very few instances would the family ask for a funeral service according to the *BCP*. Evangelical clergy may wish to consider proactively recommending the *BCP* service to families and talk through the structure and emphasis of

---

[4] A 2014 Co-Operative Funeralcare survey of 30,000 funerals revealed the most popular music at British funerals: 1. Monty Python 'Always Look on the Bright Side of Life'; 2. Traditional 'The Lord is my Shepherd'; 3. Traditional 'Abide with me'; 4. BBC TV 'Match of the Day' theme; 5. Frank Sinatra 'I did it my way.' http://www.telegraph.co.uk/news/picturegalleries/howaboutthat/11243943/Baby-boomers-jazz-up-their-funerals-with-Monty-Python-and-fancy-dress.html. Accessed 6 Feb 2015.

the service. The basic structure could be maintained whilst adding in a short personal tribute, hymns etc. Paul Thomas in his book on using the *BCP* makes the point that the burial service 'is very simple, even stark' with the departed not named at any point and there are no prayers for those who mourn.[5] Most evangelical clergy today would be happy to provide for these omissions, not seeing the *BCP* as an ossified relic. Ministers will also not want to create the universalist impression that everyone who dies will be sure and certain of resurrection to new life. This is where the sermon complements the liturgy and clears up any possible confusion – only a lively faith in Christ leads to eternal salvation. Any speculation on the eternal destiny of the departed should be avoided, unless it is abundantly clear that the funeral is for a faithful and committed Christian, and we can assure people that they are now with the Lord.

Ministers may also have the opportunity to tackle erroneous beliefs about the afterlife and damaging practices such as spiritualism and consulting mediums, which is surprisingly common in a supposedly secular society. The Bible clearly warns against divination and consulting the dead (Leviticus 20:27; Deuteronomy 18:10-14). The Roman Catholic teaching on intermediate states and the ability of the living to influence the eternal destiny of the dead can often lead people in this direction. The false hope of mediums needs to be replaced with the sure hope of the resurrected and ascended Lord Jesus. Evil forces are at work in our world and it is not impossible to raise the spirits of the dead, as the sorry tale of Saul and the witch of Endor (1 Samuel 28) teaches us – 'Samuel is recognisable, coherent and communicative'. There is no suggestion that trickery was involved – the spirit of the dead Samuel was raised.[6]

9.3. Some Principles from the BCP Burial Service

9.3.1. For the living, not the dead

The temptation and pressure at every funeral service is to focus solely on the deceased person and let their tribute overpower everything else.

---

[5] Paul Thomas, *Using the Book of Common Prayer: A Simple Guide* (London: Church House Publishing, 2012), p 133.

[6] For a helpful analysis of this narrative, see Krish Kandiah's article, http://www.christiantoday.com/article/the.undead.necromancy.and.a.really.scary.halloween.thought/68719.htm. Accessed 27 Nov 2015. Cf. Dale Ralph Davis, *1 Samuel: Looking on the Heart* (Fearn: Christian Focus, 2000), pp 289-300.

It is often helpful to see the first part of the service, of whatever length, as giving thanks for a life, then the second half expresses the Christian hope of Christ and His resurrection. The service is to help the congregation process their thoughts and feelings and gently to challenge them to respond to God's saving work of reconciliation in Christ. A funeral service that does not focus on Christ and the resurrection is a terrible missed opportunity.

9.3.2. Confidence overcomes fear

Much of medieval art and writing about death centred on the pains of Hell, with lurid Doom paintings vividly depicting the fate of those who are judged on the Last Day and found wanting. Protestant theology re-introduced the absolute confidence and assurance of the believer who is trusting wholly in the merits of Jesus Christ's death and resurrection. Many Christians still misguidedly think certainty of heaven and eternal life is presumptuous and arrogant. Rather, it is the humble and gracious gift of God to all those who have faith in Christ:

> For by grace you have been saved through faith. And this is not your own doing; it is the gift of God, not a result of works, so that no one may boast. (Ephesians 2:7-8 ESV).

9.3.3. The Bible instead of tradition

The Reformers insisted that we go back to the Scriptures for the Church's belief and practice, not simply accepting the traditions and customs that have accumulated over the centuries. The BCP Burial Service is solidly constructed from biblical passages, which outline some of the great truths of the Gospel. People attending funeral services have a huge range of fanciful and erroneous ideas concerning death and the afterlife. The Burial Service presents succinctly the truth from God's Word, as incorporated into the liturgy.

9.3.4. Jesus, our only mediator

The Medieval Church placed a huge emphasis on the mediation and intercession of Mary and the saints on behalf of the Christian believer, both living and dead. The Reformers wanted to honour the exemplary lives of prominent Christians in the past, but in no way can they intercede and influence one's eternal salvation. The Prayer Book places a wonderful emphasis on the unique and exclusive role of Christ as mediator and Saviour. Praying to intermediaries and belief in purgatory necessarily diminishes the role of Christ as Saviour and Mediator: 'For there is one God, and there is one mediator between God and men, the man Christ Jesus' (1 Timothy 2:5 ESV). He must increase and we must decrease.

Nancy Guthrie recently wrote a piece on the Gospel Coalition website entitled, 'Please Don't make my Funeral all about Me'. She comments on the all too familiar spectacle of a thanksgiving/celebration/funeral service with little mention of death and the grief that it brings – 'Christ and his saving benefits could not be made much of because death and its cruelties were largely ignored.'[7] Both the darkness of sin and death, and the light of the Gospel need to be presented. Any sanitised and idealised portrayal of the deceased is not honouring to our Maker and Redeemer and lays no foundation for the Gospel. Guthrie also helpfully suggests that our wishes for our funeral service should be clearly written down, as they are just as important as to where our worldly goods may end up. Perhaps we should teach and encourage believers in our congregations to leave instructions for a clearly Christ-focussed service and to ensure that their relatives are aware of these wishes.

9.3.5. *Simplicity rather than complexity*

The Burial Service is not long and complicated. It is not part of a huge set of rites associated with death and dying that *Common Worship* represents, going back to pre-Reformation patterns of worship and pastoral care. The *BCP* resisted the Genevan and Scottish moves to have no set liturgy at all for funerals, but instead offered a simple, unadorned service distilled from Scripture. The service as it stands is not stark, but ministers today may perfectly well use it with judicious additions, which would not detract from the integrity of the service as Cranmer intended.

---

[7] http://thegospelcoalition.org/article/please-dont-make-my-funeral-all-about-me, accessed 19/9/2014.

10. Conclusion

Death is still a taboo subject for many British people today and for most, as Paul Helm has commented, 'concern for the present life has overpowered that for the life to come'.[1] Christians have a duty and privilege to proclaim through word and deed the Gospel of our risen Lord to a fallen and lost world. The principles enshrined in the *Book of Common Prayer* remain valid for our own generation, though they must be communicated in a way people can understand and respond to. There are all manner of strange folk ideas and beliefs swirling around the idea of death and an after-life. The Burial Service does not let us dream up our own debased concept of truth. It presents to us clearly the Word of God, our Creator and Redeemer, as revealed in the pages of Holy Scripture. Therefore, we do not need to speculate about what happens after our death.

The congregation are encouraged to meditate on their own mortality and to place their trust whole-heartedly in Christ, whom God sent to be Saviour of the World. Everyone is responsible and accountable. God created us out of dust and to that same dust we return, but 'in sure and certain hope of the resurrection to eternal life'. Death for the Christian believer is a necessary stepping-stone, a door to a wonderful future with Christ, who will change our fallen, mortal body into a 'glorious body' akin to his own. The Prayer Book knows nothing of disembodied souls floating on clouds, and rejects a Platonic denigration of created, physical bodies. Cranmer's biblical acumen understood a holistic and integrated future for the Christian departed. Those who die in the Lord are truly blessed and enter into the eternal rest prepared for all of God's elect. Leaving the 'miseries of this sinful world' behind is a great joy, though it does occasion grief and mourning for loved ones left behind. Believers are already with God in 'joy and felicity', but this is only an intermediate state until they are clothed again with the resurrection body that will be part of 'the general Resurrection in the last day' when the saved and lost will enter their final eternal state. Judgment will surely follow on from death and there will be a division of humanity. On that day God's chosen people will hear Christ's pronouncement that they will 'receive the kingdom prepared for you from the beginning of the world'. The Prayer Book wants to affirm that believers who have departed this world are indeed with God now in heaven, but this is not the end of the story – the final act of the drama of redemption is yet to unfold.

---

[1] Paul Helm, *The Last Things: Death, Judgment, Heaven and Hell* (Edinburgh: Banner of Truth, 1989), p 9.

11. Appendices

11.1. Appendix 1: Cremation versus burial

11.1.1. Christian Tradition

From earliest times, Jews and Christians have wanted to bury their dead, in contrast to many cultures who routinely practised cremation. The Roman historian Tacitus saw that a distinguishing characteristic of Jews compared to the Romans is that they 'prefer to bury and not burn their dead'.[1] The extensive and laborious Roman catacombs (which contain perhaps as many as three million corpses) testify to this wish for burial. Christian burial sites were originally called *coemeteria*, literally 'sleeping places', denoting a fervent belief in a future resurrection. It is this expectation of physical resurrection that shaped much of early Christian burial practise. The last non-Christian emperor, Julian the Apostate (AD 332-363), identified care of the dead as one of the factors, together with love of neighbour and honesty, that contributed to the spread of Christianity.[2] Many of the Church Fathers wrote about burial in relation to the future hope of physical resurrection e.g. Irenaeus (*Against Heresies*, 5. 15-16), but it was only with Tertullian that we find an explicit denunciation of cremation: only the heathen 'burn up their dead with harshest inhumanity' (*On the Resurrection of the Flesh*, Ch. 1), and Tertullian's readers are urged to avoid cremation, 'a cruel custom with regard to the body since, being human, it does not deserve what is inflicted upon criminals' (*A Treatise on the Soul*, Ch. 51). Care of the body in burial was often seen as a powerful defence against those who saw the created world as inferior and sinful. The Paderborn Capitularies (AD 785) at the time of Charlemagne even went so far to declare cremation to be a capital offence.[3] Until the 19th Century criticism of cremation was the default position of the Christian Church.

Christians cared about dead bodies because the body was created by God and bore His image, and therefore worthy of respect and honour. At the Incarnation the Word took on human flesh and uniquely dignified and hallowed human physical existence. Jesus was himself

---

[1] Tacitus, *Histories*, Book V, para. 5. See Eric Rebillard, *The Care of the Dead in Late Antiquity* (Ithaca, NY: Cornell University Press, 2009).
[2] David W. Jones, 'To Bury or Burn? Toward an Ethic of Cremation.', *JETS* 53 (2010) pp 335-47, pages 337-38.
[3] Jones, 'To Bury or Burn?', pp 338-39.

buried and raised bodily from the dead. A Christian's burial was therefore a witness to the resurrection yet to come and Jesus becomes our example. The New Testament teaches that the believer's body is 'a temple of the Holy Spirit' (1 Corinthians 6:19), making them vessels worthy of honour.

The future resurrection would not be in any way inhibited or prevented by bodies being burnt, as was the case with many early martyrs. There is discontinuity as well continuity between our present earthly body and the new, perfect resurrection body. Minucius Felix (2nd Century apologist) remarked, 'We do not fear any loss from any mode of sepulture, but we adhere to the old and better custom of burial'.[4] Evangelicals have often expressed similar sentiments. Billy Graham once replied to a correspondent concerned at the recent cremation of her mother:

> It is true that cremation is of pagan tradition, but that does not necessarily make it a sinful act... I am confident that it has nothing whatever to do with the resurrection of the body. Many Christians have been accidentally burned, some were burned as martyrs, but this certainly will not limit God in the resurrection. The Bible teaches that we will have a new body in the resurrection. It appears that the actual mode of disposing of the dead is not the crucial issue and it need cause you no remorse.[5]

11.1.2. Biblical Evidence

If the weight of Christian tradition is clearly on the side of burials, the biblical evidence is more ambiguous and nowhere explicitly condemns cremation. The patriarchs showed great care and respect for the bodies of their loved ones – think of the great lengths Abraham went to in Genesis 23 to secure a tomb for his wife Sarah. It was later used for three generations of patriarchs and their wives. Joseph was also very keen that his bones should be buried in the land of Israel, and Hebrews 11:22 views this as evidence of faith.[6] We are even told in Deuteronomy 34 that God Himself buried Moses opposite Beth-Peor. This unique event is also referred to in Jude 9. Burial is always seen in a positive light, the natural

---

[4] Quoted in Timothy George, 'Cremation Confusion: Is it unscriptural for a Christian to be cremated?', *Christianity Today* 21 May (2002).
[5] Billy Graham, *My Answer* (Garden City, New York: Doubleday, 1960), p 197.
[6] See Jones, 'To Bury or Burn? Toward an Ethic of Cremation.' for further biblical discussion and references.

mode of disposing of a dead body amongst God's people. Conversely, there are examples of cremation in the Old Testament, but they are often associated with God's judgment and curse – Achan (Joshua 7:25), Saul (1 Samuel 31:12), the King of Edom (Amos 2:1).[7]

The clear respect in Jewish custom due to a dead body is also evident in the Gospel accounts, where Joseph of Arimathea's tomb and the anointing of the body of Christ as an act of love are emphasised. John 19:40 makes the point that 'the custom of the Jews is to bury', but that is a statement of fact, not a command or recommendation. Even deceitful Ananias and Sapphira are buried in Acts 5. Paul did indeed offer his body to be burned (1 Corinthians 13:3) but here he was thinking about martyrdom, not cremation.

David Jones attempts to look at the burial versus cremation debate from the perspective of ethics.[8] What constitutes love of God and love of neighbour when it comes to caring for a dead body? Are there other, theological considerations as well as expense, environment and ease of organisation? Jones makes the point that in the Bible buried corpses are referred to as named people and the most prevalent description in the New Testament to describe the death of a believer is 'sleep', a term used by Jesus (e.g. John 11:11) and by Paul (e.g. 1 Corinthians 15:6). In view of these passages, we understand that the body is more than a temporary shell inhabited for a season. The real individual must be seen as holistic, with both material and immaterial components. On death, the corpse is still deserving of respect, and the body will be reunited with soul and spirit at the end of the age (Romans 8:23). Jones emphasises the belief that for the Christian believer, a funeral is not just a means of disposing of a dead body, but a precious opportunity to remember the Christian hope of resurrection made available to us in Jesus Christ. If we want to communicate the divine value in the material world, the hope of future bodily resurrection and the promise of eternal physical existence, then many Christians would prefer burial to cremation, despite the extra expense and effort that may occasion. It is perhaps no coincidence that as the belief that death is the end of human existence grows ('I believe that when I die I shall rot' – Bertrand Russell in 1925), so does the rate of cremation. Christian burial is a powerful and very visible antidote to that prevailing mood of annihilation at death.

---

[7] See, for example, the treatment in Donald Howard, *Burial or Cremation: Does it matter?* (Edinburgh: Banner of Truth, 2001); Adrian V W Freer, *Burial or Cremation for Christians? A Biblical Pattern for Funerals* (Holywell: Evangelical Press, 2015).

[8] Jones, 'To Bury or Burn? Toward an Ethic of Cremation.'.

11.1.3. Rates of Cremation

In the 21st Century many Christians have largely abandoned the traditional preference for burial because of perceived environmental concerns (burials take up too much space), the preference of undertakers, and the growing cost of traditional burials.[9] Many people have also lost their sense of place within a local community and being buried in the churchyard or cemetery beside one's ancestors is not seen as important as it once was. In 1963 the Pope finally lifted the ban on Roman Catholics seeking cremation (whilst 'earnestly recommending' burial as the preferred practise) and today in the UK only a few religious groups, including Muslims, Orthodox Jews and the Greek and Russian Orthodox churches, still actively oppose cremation.

The figures for 2012 show that 74.3% of deaths in the UK ended in cremation although it is much more popular in England and Wales (75%) than in Scotland (34%) or Northern Ireland (17%).[10] This figure is only going to rise, as land becomes scarcer and cremations become cheaper in relation to burials. (In Japan the rate is nearly 99%, whereas in Poland with a strong Roman Catholic tradition the rate is about 9%. The United States has a rate of 40%).

Evangelical clergy today should perhaps not fixate on the actual mode of disposing of a dead body, but rather on ensuring that they can clearly present the claims of the Gospel. A modern service at a crematorium can often feel rather cold and clinical with little to help those grieving confront the reality of death or to offer the resurrection hope a traditional burial service offers. A burial service is preferable given the theological underpinning above, and it allows more space and time for reflection, healthy grieving and acknowledgement of the physicality of both death and our future bodily resurrection.

---

[9] Edwards, *After Death?*, pp 17-29.
[10] http://news.bbc.co.uk/1/hi/magazine/7963119.stm, accessed 19/9/2014. Cf. 'International Cremation Statistics', The Cremation Society of Great Britain; http://www.effs.eu/cms/fileadmin/members_only/documents/news_articles/UK_Cremation_Statistics_1960-2012.pdf. Accessed 26 November 2015. Cf. Cremation rates chart- http://www.economist.com/blogs/graphicdetail/2012/10/daily-chart-16. Accessed 20/2/15.

11.2. Appendix 2: Suicide

The rubric at the beginning of the 1662 *BCP* funeral service states, 'Here it is to be noted, that the Office ensuing is not to be used for any that die unbaptized, or excommunicate, or have laid violent hands upon themselves'. The form of burial for suicides was never given. This somewhat harsh provision has often proven difficult to many Christians, who note the acute mental turmoil and depression that can lead even committed believers to take their own lives. The appropriate canon of the Church of England, B38.2, states:

> It shall be the duty of every minister to bury, according to the rites of the Church of England, the corpse or ashes of any person deceased within his cure or of any parishioners or persons whose names are entered on the church electoral roll of his parish whether deceased within his cure or elsewhere that is brought to a church or burial ground or cemetery under his control in which the burial or interment of such corpse or ashes may lawfully be effected, due notice being given; except the person deceased have died unbaptized, or being of sound mind have laid violent hands upon himself, or have been declared excommunicate for some grievous and notorious crime and no man to testify to his repentance; in which case and in any other case at the request of the relative, friend, or legal representative having charge of or being responsible for the burial he shall use at the burial such service as may be prescribed or approved by the Ordinary, being a service neither contrary to, nor indicative of any departure from, the doctrine of the Church of England in any essential matter: Provided that, if a form of service available for the burial of suicides is approved by the General Synod under Canon B 2, that service shall be used where applicable instead of the aforesaid service prescribed or approved by the Ordinary, unless the person having charge or being responsible for the burial otherwise requests.

The *BCP* exception has been altered to include 'being of sound mind', an acknowledgement that people committing suicide are frequently not of sound mind.[11]

---

[11] MacDonald and Murphy, *Sleepless Souls*, p 16. Fewer than 2% of suicides between 1485 and 1660 were judged to be *non compos mentis* i.e. not guilty of the serious crime of suicide.

11.2.1. *The Crime of Self-Murder*

The contemporary sympathy towards suicide is not to downplay the strong Christian tradition that suicide is always sinful and violates the sixth commandment, 'You shall not murder', Exodus 20:13 (NRSV), though many other translations, including the AV, Tyndale, Geneva, have 'kill' instead of 'murder'. The example of Samson's death in Judges 16 proved controversial. Augustine assumed that he must have had a secret command of God, but the Puritan William Ames, though citing Samson to prove that suicide was forbidden (the Bible never says so explicitly) says, 'it is lawful... sometimes to expose oneself to such a danger, by which death must necessarily though indirectly follow'.[12] Classical and early Christians are frequently quoted in debates precisely because the scriptural prohibitions against suicide seemed weak. The Roman Catholic Church used to deny the funeral Mass and burial to suicides, as it was a mortal sin, but that was relaxed in 1983. The Catechism of the Catholic Church, 2282/83, states,

> Grave psychological disturbances, anguish, or grave fear of hardship, suffering, or torture can diminish the responsibility of the one committing suicide. We should not despair of the eternal salvation of persons who have taken their own lives. By ways known to him alone, God can provide the opportunity for salutary repentance. The Church prays for persons who have taken their own lives.[13]

It should also be noted that early in the Christian tradition people were seen as martyrs if they killed themselves to avoid a worse fate. Augustine discusses suicide in detail in his *City of God*, Book 1, chapters 16-23 and although he has great sympathy particularly for Christian women who killed themselves to avoid rape, suicide is sinful and breaking God's law. Aquinas[14] later defended this prohibition on three grounds:

(1) Suicide is contrary to natural self-love, whose aim is to preserve us,
(2) Suicide injures the community of which an individual is a part,
(3) Suicide violates our duty to God because God has given us life as a gift and in taking our lives we violate His right to determine the duration of our earthly existence.

---

[12] Quoted in MacDonald and Murphy, *Sleepless Souls*, p 93.
[13] http://www.vatican.va/archive/ccc_css/archive/catechism/p3s2c2a5.htm, accessed 22 October 2014.
[14] Thomas Aquinas, *Summa Theologica,* 2nd part of the 2nd Part, Q64 Article 5.

At the Reformation there was 'intensified religious hostility to self-murder' compared to the previous medieval period and the later post-Enlightenment era.[15] Suicide was often linked to the direct temptations of Satan so that, according to Hugh Latimer, 'they rid themselves out of this life; but this is not well done'.[16] Thomas Beard's popular and influential *Theatre of God's Judgements* (1597) showed many instances of a guilty conscience ultimately leading to the sinner taking their own life, where Satan is an agent of God's wrath. For Beard, suicide was often more a case of divine retribution than of diabolical temptation.[17] The English Reformers were unanimous in following Augustine and Aquinas that suicide was sinful, and suffering, even unto death, was not a reason to take one's life, thus breaking the commandment against killing and usurping God's rightful authority over human life. William Whitaker, for example, could write in 1610, 'the Holy Spirit judges not of valour by the same measures of profane men, who extol Cato to the skies for committing suicide'.[18] The Westminster Shorter Catechism, which remains authoritative for many Reformed believers, follows in a similar vein: 'The sixth commandment forbids the taking away of our own life, or the life of our neighbour unjustly, or anything tending to it.'[19] The future Archbishop of Canterbury, George Abbot summed up much Protestant opinion when he declared in 1600 that suicide was 'a sin so grievous that scant any is more heinous unto the Lord'. Lancelot Andrewes was certainly not as Reformed as Abbot, but he could still say of self-killing, 'It is worse than beastly to kill or drown or make away with ourselves; for... the very swine would not have run into the sea but that they were carried by the devil'.[20] Richard Sibbes noted that ungodly men sank deeper and deeper into despair until they killed themselves,

---

[15] MacDonald and Murphy, *Sleepless Souls*, p 2.

[16] George Elwes Corrie (ed.), *Sermons by Hugh Latimer* (Cambridge: Parker Society, Cambridge University Press, 1844), Vol. 1, p 435.

[17] Alexandra Walsham, *Providence in Early Modern England* (Oxford: Oxford University Press, 1999), pp 65-115; MacDonald and Murphy, *Sleepless Souls*, p 33. Beard often copied Foxe's examples of papist persecutors of English Protestants, who subsequently killed themselves.

[18] William Whitaker, *A Disputation on Holy Scripture Against the Papists, Especially Bellarmine and Stapleton*. William Fitzgerald (Ed.) (Cambridge: Parker Society/Cambridge University Press, 1849), p 95. Also, Henry Bullinger, *Decades*. Ed. Thomas Harding (Cambridge: Parker Society/ Cambridge University Press, 1850), Vol. 2, pp 414-15; Bradford, *Writings*. Ed. Aubrey Townsend, Vol. 1, p 61.

[19] Thomas F. Torrance (ed.), *The School of Faith: The Catechisms of the Reformed Church* (London: James Clark & Co., 1959), p 272.

[20] Quoted in MacDonald and Murphy, *Sleepless Souls*, pp 31-32.

whereas godly men could learn the 'art or skill of bearing troubles... that it weigheth not over heavy.'[21] The allegorical tradition with Christian hope battling suicidal desperation can be seen in Spenser's *Faerie Queene* (1590) and Bunyan's *Pilgrim Progress* (1678). As MacDonald and Murphy comment, 'The symbolic association of Satan, apostasy, despair, and suicide was implanted in the Protestant mind'.[22]

11.2.2. Calvin

Calvin will have nothing to do with the Stoic notion of noble death exemplified in Cato and others. Calvin reiterated Aquinas' natural law argument that all things love themselves and even the most savage beasts try to preserve the state in which God placed them. Such an unnatural act was so extreme that suicides are 'possessed by the devil' in suppressing the self-preservation instinct, something that by the late Middle Ages was a commonplace in Christian thinking, but had not been present in Augustine or Aquinas.[23] It is worthwhile noting that Calvin's repugnance for suicide is, uncharacteristically, not driven by biblical exegesis, as the Bible does not clearly condemn voluntary death. Calvin also did not touch on the subject in his exposition of the Commandments, discussing only interpersonal violence.[24] Jeffrey Watt comments that Calvin rarely dealt with suicide in his works and it is not mentioned in any editions of the *Institutes*. He does touch on the subject of self-murder in sermons on Saul (1 Samuel 31) and Ahithophel (2 Samuel 17). 'The central argument that Calvin made against suicide is that in taking one's life, one is disobedient by refusing to submit to the will of God. God has given life to humans; God alone has the right to take it away.'[25] Using Pythagoras' old analogy, Calvin preached that we are all like soldiers on sentry duty and we must not leave our post until the commander orders us. Even King Saul's wish not to fall into the hands of the Philistines was a sinful example of not being willing to suffer as part of God's will.

---

[21] Richard Sibbes, *The Complete Works*. Ed. A. B. Grosart (Edinburgh: 1862-4), Vol. 1, p 148.
[22] MacDonald and Murphy, *Sleepless Souls*, p 40.
[23] Jeffrey R. Watt, 'Calvin on Suicide', *Church History* 66 (1997) pp 463-76, 469.
[24] It is worth noting that according to contemporary records suicide was rare compared to, say, infanticide. Between Calvin's return to Geneva in 1541 and his death in 1564 there were only eight suicides in the city and three in the surrounding countryside. Watt, 'Calvin on Suicide', p 476.
[25] Watt, 'Calvin on Suicide', quote p 465.

The bodies of suicides were still desecrated in Geneva, being dragged around the town, impaled and either left exposed in the open, or buried in ignominious ground, such an execution site. It would seem that Calvin, not wishing to give meaning to burial of the body, acquiesced to these popular practices as deeply entrenched in Christian society.

The first comprehensive modern defence of suicide was John Donne's *Biathanatos* (c. 1607). Not intended for publication, but published posthumously in 1647, *Biathanatos* drew upon an array of classical and modern legal and theological sources to argue that Christian doctrine should not hold that suicide is necessarily sinful. His critique is in effect internal, drawing upon the logic of Christian thought itself to suggest that suicide is not contrary to the laws of nature, of reason, or of God. Were it contrary to the law of nature mandating self-preservation, all acts of self-denial or privation would be similarly unlawful. Moreover, there may be circumstances in which reason might recommend suicide. Finally, Donne observes, not only does Biblical Scripture lack a clear condemnation of suicide, Christian doctrine has permitted other forms of killing such as martyrdom, capital punishment and killing in wartime.[26] Donne was an isolated voice on the issue, flying contrary to the consensus of Christian thinking on the subject and it wasn't until the full flowering of the Enlightenment in the 18th Century that suicide could be seen as legitimate and perhaps the ultimate form of self-expression.

11.2.3. Suicidal Melancholy

Critics of Protestant 'enthusiasm' and Puritan excess often attributed their conduct to melancholy, a common medical imbalance of the humours, which could lead to delusions, madness and even suicide.[27] Whereas Robert Burton in his famous 'Anatomy of Melancholy' (1621) echoed the conventional indictments of Puritan zeal, which was the result of ignorance or hypocrisy, albeit with the possibility of

---

[26] Stanford Encyclopedia of Philosophy, 'Suicide'. http://plato.stanford.edu/entries/suicide/, accessed 22 October 2014.

[27] John F. Sena, 'Melancholic Madness and the Puritans', *The Harvard Theological Review* 66 (1973) pp 293-309. Cf. Alexandra Walsham, "Frantick Hacket': Prophecy, Sorcery, Insanity, and the Elizabethan Puritan Movement', *The Historical Journal* 41 (1998) pp 27-66, especially pp 48-49; Michael P. Winship, 'Puritans, Politics, and Lunacy: The Coppinger-Hacket Conspiracy as the Apotheosis of Elizabethan Puritanism', *The Sixteenth Century Journal* 38 (2007) pp 345-69.

contributory psychological and physiological disorders, Meric Casaubon, in 'A Treatise Concerning Enthusiasm' (1656), did not impugn the sincerity of the Puritans, but did see melancholy behind enthusiasts thinking of themselves as divinely inspired. Melancholic vapours could cause a person to have apparitions and delusions that seemed to be supernaturally inspired as from Heaven. This became an important element in the Conformists' defence against Puritan nonconformity.

Puritans themselves were interested in melancholy as a serious impediment to a godly life and noted that suicide was often a temptation to be overcome.[28] Richard Baxter recognised the seriousness of melancholy, noting in a sermon of 1682 that it 'could swallow up faith' and lead to despair and worse. Reason could be corrupted, false delusions could occur and he recommended some of the standard medical antidotes for melancholy.[29] 'A Pious, Credible woman' told Richard Baxter that one day when she was unhappy the devil had appeared in her parlour in the shape of a big black man, holding a noose in his hand and pointing to the lintel.[30]

Some saw the rise of religious despair resulting from melancholy as the reason for the rise of suicide in England in the early 18th Century. As Sena comments, 'the theory and terminology for popular attacks on the Puritans came largely from medical treatises of the seventeenth and eighteenth centuries'.[31] Opponents began to charge that excessive Puritan emphasis on election could also drive pious men and women to despair and self-destruction. A morbid preoccupation with sin was indeed a by-product of some Puritan preaching, but spiritual turmoil was often given a positive spiritual meaning. MacDonald and Murphy perhaps overstate their case by remarking, 'The Puritans thus, in effect, institutionalised suicidal moods, presenting them as the emotional

---

[28] See for instance 'A Sweet Comfort for an Afflicted Conscience' by Richard Greenham, *Works,* ed. Henry Holland (London, 1599), pp 233-79.
[29] Quoted in Sena, 'Melancholic Madness and the Puritans', p 302.
[30] Quoted in Michael MacDonald, 'The Secularization of Suicide in England 1660-1800', *Past & Present* 111 (1986) pp 50-100, page 55.
[31] Sena, 'Melancholic Madness and the Puritans', p 307. Joseph Addison in 1712 denounced the Puritans 'of a sorrowful countenance, and generally eaten up with spleen and melancholy'. They wanted to look sad, looking 'on a sudden fit of laughter, as a breach of his baptismal vow'. Addison saw such behaviour as dissuading against all religion. Contemplating God should lead to joy and cheerfulness. 'By the 1750s, all manifestations of charismatic Protestantism were being stigmatized as species of madness – the equation of religious enthusiasm with insanity had become a ruling-class shibboleth': Walsham, "Frantick Hacket", p 61.

symbol of the luminal stage between the sinful life and regeneration'. Puritans such as Sibbes resented these sorts of accusations and stated that joy should be the true character of the Christian.[32]

11.2.4. Pastoral Care

Common Worship 'Pastoral Services' includes explicit prayers for 'After a suicide' (p 360) and makes the very valid point that the manner of death should not cloud the good memories of the person's life and we must pray for those who can see nothing but despair and darkness. Ultimately, nothing can separate us from the love of Christ (Romans 8:39). The minister conducting the funeral of a suicide has to contend not just with the extraordinary sensitivities of the occasion and the guilt of many of the family and friends, but also with the canon law of the Church of England. A General Synod Private Member's Motion (12 February 2015) on Canon B38 amended the canon to allow 'those who have taken their own life, whatever the circumstances, to be buried in accordance with the rites of the Church of England'.[33] Clergy routinely conduct services of suicides using the *Book of Common Prayer* and *Common Worship*, but were technically breaking the existing canon law in doing so. Many relatives still believe that 'the Church' disapproves of suicide, that it is unforgiveable, and burials will not be permitted in churchyards. The motion sought to bring canon law into line with has been happening 'on the ground' for many years. Public sympathies and a greater understanding of mental health led to legislation in 1961 abolishing the offence of suicide.

The minister could perhaps take particular care with the penitential nature of the service, leaving space and time for the congregation to confess their sins before God, asking His forgiveness through Christ. Many will want to acknowledge that they could have done more to prevent the suicide, yet this has to be balanced with both the recognition that the person who killed themselves may not have been 'of sound mind', and much guilt may be misplaced. A compassionate, loving God,

---

[32] MacDonald and Murphy, *Sleepless Souls*, p 65.
[33] Church of England, General Synod papers GS 1972A, GS 1972B. https://www.churchofengland.org/media/2141164/gs%201972b%20-%20pmm%20on%20canon%20b%2038.pdf. Accessed 28 November 2015. The vote was passed (262 for, 5 against, 6 abstentions) in General Synod to remove the ban on funeral of suicides. For the text of the helpful debate, see GS proceedings: https://www.churchofengland.org/media/2265845/rop%20feb%202015%20%28final%20indexed%20version%29.pdf

who is with us in our sorrow and grief, longing for us to turn to Him, is a helpful focus. For some pointers on preaching at funerals of suicides, see the helpful volume of sermons edited by Bryan Chapell.[34]

---

[34] Bryan Chapell (ed.), *The Hardest Sermons you'll ever have to Preach* (Grand Rapids, MI: Zondervan, 2011), pp 227-73, reading list p 281. For recent UK suicide statistics, see the Samaritans publication 'Suicide Statistics Report 2014': http://www.samaritans.org/sites/default/files/kcfinder/files/research/Samaritans%20Suicide%20Statistics%20Report%202014.pdf.

12. Bibliography

ACUTE, *The Nature of Hell: A Report by the Evangelical Alliance Commission on Unity and Truth Among Evangelicals (ACUTE)*, Carlisle: ACUTE/ Paternoster, 2000.

Althaus, Paul, *The Theology of Martin Luther*, Philadelphia: Fortress Press, 1966.

Atherstone, Andrew, *Charles Simeon on the Excellency of the Liturgy*, Joint Liturgical Studies 72, Norwich: Alcuin Club/ The Group for Renewal of Worship, 2011.

Bennett, Arthur, 'Prayer for the Departed', *Churchman* 81, (1967) 4, 252-64.

Blunt, John Henry (ed.), *The Annotated Book of Common Prayer, being an historical, ritual, and theological commentary on the devotional system of the Church of England*, rev. edn., London: Rivingtons, 1884.

Bradford, John, *Writings*. Ed. Aubrey Townsend, 2 vols, Cambridge: Parker Society/ Cambridge University Press, 1848-53.

Bray, Gerald (ed.), *Tudor Church Reform: The Henrician Canons of 1535 and the Reformatio Legum Ecclesiasticarum*, Church of England Record Society 8, Woodbridge: The Boydell Press, 2000.

Bray, Gerald, *The Faith we Confess: An Exposition of the Thirty-Nine Articles*, London: The Latimer Trust, 2009.

Buchanan, Colin, *The Savoy Conference Revisited*, Joint Liturgical Studies 54, Cambridge: The Alcuin Club/ The Group for Renewal of Worship, 2002.

Bullinger, Henry, *Decades*. Ed. Thomas Harding, 4 vols, Cambridge: Parker Society/ Cambridge University Press, 1850.

Burgess, Clive, "Longing to be prayed for': death and commemoration in an English parish in the later Middle Ages' in Gordon, Bruce and Marshall, Peter (eds.), *The Place of the Dead: Death and Remembrance in Late Medieval and Early Modern Europe* (Cambridge: Cambridge University Press, 2000) 44-65.

Calvin, John, *Selected Works of John Calvin: Tracts and Letters*. Henry Beveridge and Jules Bonnet (eds.), 7 vols, Grand Rapids, MI: Baker, 1983.

Cameron, Euan, *The European Reformation*, Oxford: The Clarendon Press, 2000.

Cameron, Euan, *The European Reformation*, 2nd. edn., Oxford: Oxford University Press, 2012.

Cardwell, Edward, *A History of Conferences and Other Proceedings Connected with the Revision of the Book of Common Prayer; from the year 1558 to the Year 1690* 3rd. edn., Oxford: Oxford University Press, 1849.

Chapell, Bryan (ed.), *The Hardest Sermons you'll ever have to Preach*, Grand Rapids, MI: Zondervan, 2011.

Corrie, George Elwes (ed.), *Sermons by Hugh Latimer*, Cambridge: Parker Society, Cambridge University Press, 1844.

Craig, H. R. M., 'Prayer and the Departed', *Churchman* 86, (1972) 3, 201-04.

Cranmer, Thomas, *Miscellaneous Writings and Letters of Thomas Cranmer*. John Edmund Cox (Ed.), Cambridge: Parker Society/Cambridge University Press, 1846.

BIBLIOGRAPHY

Cressy, David, *Birth, Marriage & Death: Ritual, Religion, and the Life-Cycle in Tudor and Stuart England*, Oxford: Oxford University Press, 1997.

Cuming, Geoffrey, *The Godly Order: Texts and Studies relating to the Book of Common Prayer*, London: Alcuin Club/ SPCK, 1983.

Davis, Dale Ralph, *1 Samuel: Looking on the Heart*, Fearn: Christian Focus, 2000.

Duffy, Eamon, *The Stripping of the Altars: Traditional Religion in England c.1400 - c.1580*, New Haven: Yale University Press, 1992.

Duffy, Eamon, 'The Shock of Change: Continuity and Discontinuity in the Elizabethan Church of England' in Platten, Stephen (ed.), *Anglicanism and the Western Christian Tradition: Continuity, Change and the Search for Communion* (Norwich: Canterbury Press, 2003) 42-64.

Duke, Alastair, Lewis, Gillian and Pettegree, Andrew (eds.), *Calvinism in Europe, 1540-1610: A collection of Documents*, Manchester: Manchester University Press, 1992.

Edwards, David L., *After Death? Past Beliefs and Real Possibilities*, Contemporary Christian Insights, London: Continuum, 1999.

England, Church of, *Sermons, or Homilies, Appointed to be Read in Churches*, London: Prayer-Book and Homily Society, 1833.

Freer, Adrian V W, *Burial or Cremation for Christians? A Biblical Pattern for Funerals*, Holywell: Evangelical Press, 2015.

Frere, W. H. and Douglas, C. E. (eds.), *Puritan Manifestoes: A Study of the Origin of the Puritan Revolt*, London: S.P.C.K. for Church Historical Society, 1907.

Frith, John, *The Work of John Frith*. (Ed. N. T. Wright), The Courtenay Library of Reformation Classics 7, Appleford: Sutton Courtenay Press, 1983.

George, Timothy, 'Cremation Confusion: Is it unscriptural for a Christian to be cremated?', *Christianity Today* 21 May, (2002)

Gibson, Edgar Charles Sumner, *The Thirty-Nine Articles of the Church of England*. (8th Ed.), London: Methuen & Co., 1912.

Gordon, Bruce, 'Malevolent ghosts and ministering angels: apparitions and pastoral care in the Swiss Reformation' in Gordon, Bruce and Marshall, Peter (eds.), *The Place of the Dead: Death and Remembrance in Late Medieval and Early Modern Europe* (Cambridge: Cambridge University Press, 2000) 87-109.

Gordon, Bruce and Marshall, Peter, 'Introduction: placing the dead in late medieval and early modern Europe' in Gordon, Bruce and Marshall, Peter (eds.), *The Place of the Dead: Death and Remembrance in Late Medieval and early Modern Europe* (Cambridge: Cambridge University Press, 2000) 1-16.

Graham, Billy, *My Answer*, Garden City, New York: Doubleday, 1960.

Griffith Thomas, W. H., *The Principles of Theology. An introduction to the Thirty-Nine Articles*, 6th. edn., London: Vine Books, 1978.

Grindal, Edmund, *The Remains of Edmund Grindal D.D.* (Ed. William Nicholson), Cambridge: Cambridge University Press/ Parker Society, 1843.

Hague, Dyson, *Through the Prayer Book: An Exposition*, London: Church Book Room Press, 1948.

Hardwick, Charles, *A History of the Articles of Religion*, 3rd. edn., London: George Bell & Sons, 1888.

Haroutunian, Joseph (ed.), *Calvin: Commentaries,* The Library of Christian Classics XXIII, London: SCM, 1958.

Helm, Paul, *The Last Things: Death, Judgment, Heaven and Hell,* Edinburgh: Banner of Truth, 1989.

Horton, R. Anne, *Using Common Worship: Funerals. A Practical Guide to the new Services.,* London: Church House Publishing, 2000.

Houlbrooke, Ralph, 'The Puritan Death-bed, c.1560- c.1660' in Durston, Christopher and Eales, Jacqueline (eds.), *The Culture of English Puritanism, 1560-1700* (Basingstoke: Macmillan, 1996) 122-44.

Houlbrooke, Ralph, *Death, Religion and the Family in England, 1480-1750,* Oxford Studies in Social History, Oxford: Oxford University Press, 1998.

Howard, Donald, *Burial or Cremation: Does it matter?,* Edinburgh: Banner of Truth, 2001.

Hutton, Ronald, *The Rise and Fall of Merry England: The Ritual Year 1400-1700,* Oxford: Oxford University Press, 1994.

Jackson, John Frazier, 'The *Reformatio legum ecclesiasticarum*: Politics, Society, and Belief in mid-Tudor England', unpublished DPhil. thesis, Oxford University, 2003.

Jewel, John, *The Works of John Jewel.* John Ayre (ed.), 4 vols, Cambridge: Parker Society/ Cambridge University Press, 1845-1850.

Johnston, Philip S., *Shades of Sheol: Death and Afterlife in the Old Testament,* Nottingham: IVP, 2002.

Jones, David W., 'To Bury or Burn? Toward an Ethic of Cremation.', *JETS* 53, (2010) 2, 335-47.

Joynson-Hicks, William, *The Prayer Book Crisis,* London: Putnam, 1928.

Koslofsky, Craig M., *The Reformation of the Dead: Death and Ritual in Early Modern Germany, 1450-1700,* Early Modern History: Society and Culture, Basingstoke: Palgrave, 2000.

Lowther Clarke, W. K., *The New Prayer Book Explained,* rev. edn., London: SPCK, 1927.

MacCulloch, Diarmaid, *Thomas Cranmer: A Life,* New Haven; London: Yale University Press, 1996.

MacCulloch, Diarmaid, *Reformation: Europe's house divided 1490-1700,* London: Penguin, 2004.

MacDonald, Michael, 'The Secularization of Suicide in England 1660-1800', *Past & Present* 111, (1986) May, 50-100.

MacDonald, Michael and Murphy, Terence R., *Sleepless Souls: Suicide in Early Modern England,* Oxford Studies in Social History, Oxford: Oxford University Press, 1990.

Marshall, Peter, "The map of God's word': geographies of the afterlife in Tudor and early Stuart England' in Gordon, Bruce and Marshall, Peter (eds.), *The Place of the Dead: Death and Remembrance in Late Medieval and Early Modern Europe* (Cambridge: Cambridge University Press, 2000) 110-30.

Maxwell, William D., *The Liturgical Portions of the Genevan Service Book, used by John Knox while a minister of the English congregation of Marian exiles at Geneva, 1556-1559,* Edinburgh: The Faith Press Ltd., 1965.

BIBLIOGRAPHY

McGrath, Alister, *Christianity's Dangerous Idea: The Protestant Revolution. A History from the sixteenth century to the twenty-first.*, London: SPCK, 2007.

Milward, Peter, *Religious Controversies of the Elizabethan Age: A Survey of Printed Sources*, Lincoln, Neb. ; London: University of Nebraska Press, 1977.

Motyer, Alec, *After Death*, 2nd. edn., Fearn: Christian Focus, 1996.

Mounce, William D., *Pastoral Epistles*, Word Biblical Commentary, Nashville, TN: Thomas Nelson, 2000.

Neil, Charles and Willoughby, J. M. (eds.), *The Tutorial Prayer Book*, London: Church Book Room Press, 1959.

Patterson, Mary Hampson, *Domesticating the Reformation: Protestant Best Sellers, Private Devotion, and the Revolution of English Piety*, Madison, NJ: Fairleigh Dickinson University Press, 2007.

Peel, Albert (ed.), *The Seconde Parte of a Register: Being a Calendar of Manuscripts under that Title intended for Publication by the Puritans about 1593, and now in Dr. Williams's Library, London* Cambridge: Cambridge University Press, 1915.

Phillips, David, 'What should we pray? Prayer for the dead in Anglican liturgy', *Crossway* Autumn (2007) No. 106,

Pilkington, James, *The Works of John Pilkington, BD.* (ed. James Scholefield), Cambridge: Cambridge University Press/ Parker Society, 1842.

Rebillard, Eric, *The Care of the Dead in Late Antiquity*, Ithaca, NY: Cornell University Press, 2009.

Rowell, Geoffrey, *The Liturgy of Christian Burial*, Alcuin Club Collections 59, London: Alcuin Club/ SPCK, 1977.

Ryrie, Alec, *Being Protestant in Reformation Britain*, Oxford: Oxford University Press, 2013.

Sena, John F., 'Melancholic Madness and the Puritans', *The Harvard Theological Review* 66, (1973) 3, 293-309.

Sibbes, Richard, *The Complete Works*. Ed. A. B. Grosart, 7 vols, Edinburgh: 1862-4.

Spalding, James C., *The Reformation of the Ecclesiastical Laws of England, 1552*, Sixteenth Century Essays and Studies XIX, Kirksville, MO: Sixteenth Century Journal Publishers, 1992.

Spinks, Bryan D., 'Treasures Old and New: A Look at Some of Thomas Cranmer's Methods of Liturgical Compilation' in Ayris, Paul and Selwyn, David (eds.), *Thomas Cranmer: Churchman and Scholar* (Woodbridge: The Boydell Press, 1993) 175-88.

Spurr, John, *English Puritanism, 1603-1689*, Basingstoke: Macmillan, 1998.

Stannard, David E., *The Puritan way of Death: A Study in Religion, Culture, and Social Change*, New York: Oxford University Press, 1977.

Stott, John and Edwards, David L., *Essentials: A Liberal-Evangelical Dialogue*, London: Hodder & Stoughton, 1988.

Thomas, Paul, *Using the Book of Common Prayer: A Simple Guide*, London: Church House Publishing, 2012.

Torrance, Thomas F. (ed.), *The School of Faith: The Catechisms of the Reformed Church*, London: James Clark & Co., 1959.

Walsham, Alexandra, "'Frantick Hacket': Prophecy, Sorcery, Insanity, and the Elizabethan Puritan Movement', *The Historical Journal* 41, (1998) 1, 27-66.
Walsham, Alexandra, *Providence in Early Modern England*, Oxford: Oxford University Press, 1999.
Warren, F. E., *Prayer-Book Commentary for Teachers and Students*, 2nd. edn., London: SPCK, 1933.
Watt, Jeffrey R., 'Calvin on Suicide', *Church History* 66, (1997) 3, 463-76.
Whitaker, E. C., *Martin Bucer and the Book of Common Prayer*, Alcuin Club Collections 55, Great Wakering: The Alcuin Club, 1974.
Whitaker, William, *A Disputation on Holy Scripture Against the Papists, Especially Bellarmine and Stapleton*. William Fitzgerald (Ed.), Cambridge: Parker Society/Cambridge University Press, 1849.
Winship, Michael P., 'Puritans, Politics, and Lunacy: The Coppinger-Hacket Conspiracy as the Apotheosis of Elizabethan Puritanism', *The Sixteenth Century Journal* 38, (2007) 2, 345-69.
Wright, N. T., *For all the Saints? Remembering the Christian Departed*, London: SPCK, 2003.

If you have enjoyed this book, you might like to consider

- *supporting the work of the Latimer Trust*
- *reading more of our publications*
- *recommending them to others*

See *www.latimertrust.org for more information.*

Latimer Publications

Latimer Studies

LS 01	The Evangelical Anglican Identity Problem	Jim Packer
LS 02	The ASB Rite A Communion: A Way Forward	Roger Beckwith
LS 03	The Doctrine of Justification in the Church of England	Robin Leaver
LS 04	Justification Today: The Roman Catholic and Anglican Debate	R. G. England
LS 05/06	Homosexuals in the Christian Fellowship	David Atkinson
LS 07	Nationhood: A Christian Perspective	O. R. Johnston
LS 08	Evangelical Anglican Identity: Problems and Prospects	Tom Wright
LS 09	Confessing the Faith in the Church of England Today	Roger Beckwith
LS 10	A Kind of Noah's Ark? The Anglican Commitment to Comprehensiveness	Jim Packer
LS 11	Sickness and Healing in the Church	Donald Allister
LS 12	Rome and Reformation Today: How Luther Speaks to the New Situation	James Atkinson
LS 13	Music as Preaching: Bach, Passions and Music in Worship	Robin Leaver
LS 14	Jesus Through Other Eyes: Christology in a Multi-faith Context	Christopher Lamb
LS 15	Church and State Under God	James Atkinson,
LS 16	Language and Liturgy	Gerald Bray, Steve Wilcockson, Robin Leaver
LS 17	Christianity and Judaism: New Understanding, New Relationship	James Atkinson
LS 18	Sacraments and Ministry in Ecumenical Perspective	Gerald Bray
LS 19	The Functions of a National Church	Max Warren
LS19 (2nd ed.)	British Values and the National Church: Essays on Church and State from 1964-2014	Ed. David Holloway
LS 20/21	The Thirty-Nine Articles: Their Place and Use Today	Jim Packer, Roger Beckwith
LS 22	How We Got Our Prayer Book	T.W. Drury, Roger Beckwith
LS 23/24	Creation or Evolution: a False Antithesis?	Mike Poole, Gordon Wenham
LS 25	Christianity and the Craft	Gerard Moate
LS 26	ARCIC II and Justification	Alister McGrath
LS 27	The Challenge of the Housechurches	Tony Higton, Gilbert Kirby
LS 28	Communion for Children? The Current Debate	A. A. Langdon
LS 29/30	Theological Politics	Nigel Biggar
LS 31	Eucharistic Consecration in the First Four Centuries and its Implications for Liturgical Reform	Nigel Scotland
LS 32	A Christian Theological Language	Gerald Bray
LS 33	Mission in Unity: The Bible and Missionary Structures	Duncan McMann
LS 34	Stewards of Creation: Environmentalism in the Light of Biblical Teaching	Lawrence Osborn
LS 35/36	Mission and Evangelism in Recent Thinking: 1974-1986	Robert Bashford
LS 37	Future Patterns of Episcopacy: Reflections in Retirement	Stuart Blanch
LS 38	Christian Character: Jeremy Taylor and Christian Ethics Today	David Scott
LS 39	Islam: Towards a Christian Assessment	Hugh Goddard
LS 40	Liberal Catholicism: Charles Gore and the Question of Authority	G. F. Grimes
LS 41/42	The Christian Message in a Multi-faith Society	Colin Chapman
LS 43	The Way of Holiness 1: Principles	D. A. Ousley
LS 44/45	The Lambeth Articles	V. C. Miller

Latimer Publications

LS 46	The Way of Holiness 2: Issues	D. A. Ousley
LS 47	Building Multi-Racial Churches	John Root
LS 48	Episcopal Oversight: A Case for Reform	David Holloway
LS 49	Euthanasia: A Christian Evaluation	Henk Jochemsen
LS 50/51	The Rough Places Plain: AEA 1995	
LS 52	A Critique of Spirituality	John Pearce
LS 53/54	The Toronto Blessing	Martyn Percy
LS 55	The Theology of Rowan Williams	Garry Williams
LS 56/57	Reforming Forwards? The Process of Reception and the Consecration of Woman as Bishops	Peter Toon
LS 58	The Oath of Canonical Obedience	Gerald Bray
LS 59	The Parish System: The Same Yesterday, Today And For Ever?	Mark Burkill
LS 60	'I Absolve You': Private Confession and the Church of England	Andrew Atherstone
LS 61	The Water and the Wine: A Contribution to the Debate on Children and Holy Communion	Roger Beckwith, Andrew Daunton-Fear
LS 62	Must God Punish Sin?	Ben Cooper
LS 63	Too Big For Words? The Transcendence of God and Finite Human Speech	Mark D. Thompson
LS 64	A Step Too Far: An Evangelical Critique of Christian Mysticism	Marian Raikes
LS 65	The New Testament and Slavery: Approaches and Implications	Mark Meynell
LS 66	The Tragedy of 1662: The Ejection and Persecution of the Puritans	Lee Gatiss
LS 67	Heresy, Schism & Apostasy	Gerald Bray
LS 68	Paul in 3D: Preaching Paul as Pastor, Story-teller and Sage	Ben Cooper
LS69	Christianity and the Tolerance of Liberalism: J.Gresham Machen and the Presbyterian Controversy of 1922-1937	Lee Gatiss
LS70	An Anglican Evangelical Identity Crisis: The Churchman–Anvil Affair of 1981-4	Andrew Atherstone
LS71	Empty and Evil: The worship of other faiths in 1 Corinthians 8-10 and today	Rohintan Mody
LS72	To Plough or to Preach: Mission Strategies in New Zealand during the 1820s	Malcolm Falloon
LS73	Plastic People: How Queer Theory is changing us	Peter Sanlon
LS74	Deification and Union with Christ: Salvation in Orthodox and Reformed thought	Slavko Eždenci
LS75	As It Is Written: Interpreting the Bible with Boldness	Benjamin Sargent
LS76	Light From Dark Ages? An Evangelical Critique of Celtic Spirituality	Marian Raikes
LS77	The Ethics of Usury	Ben Cooper
LS78	For Us and For Our Salvation: 'Limited Atonement' in the Bible, Doctrine, History and Ministry	Lee Gatiss
LS79	Positive Complementarianism: The Key Biblical Texts	Ben Cooper
LS80	Were they Preaching 'Another Gospel'? Justification by faith in the Second Century	Andrew Daunton-Fear
LS81	Thinking Aloud: Responding to the Contemporary Debate about Marriage, Sexuality and Reconciliation	Martin Davie
LS82	Spells, Sorcerers and Spirits: Magic and the Occult in the Bible	Kirsten Birkett

Latimer Publications

Latimer Briefings

LB01	*The Church of England: What it is, and what it stands for*	R. T. Beckwith
LB02	*Praying with Understanding: Explanations of Words and Passages in the Book of Common Prayer*	R. T. Beckwith
LB03	*The Failure of the Church of England? The Church, the Nation and the Anglican Communion*	A. Pollard
LB04	*Towards a Heritage Renewed*	H.R.M. Craig
LB05	*Christ's Gospel to the Nations: The Heart & Mind of Evangelicalism Past, Present & Future*	Peter Jensen
LB06	*Passion for the Gospel: Hugh Latimer (1485–1555) Then and Now. A commemorative lecture to mark the 450th anniversary of his martyrdom in Oxford*	A. McGrath
LB07	*Truth and Unity in Christian Fellowship*	Michael Nazir-Ali
LB08	*Unworthy Ministers: Donatism and Discipline Today*	Mark Burkill
LB09	*Witnessing to Western Muslims: A Worldview Approach to Sharing Faith*	Richard Shumack
LB10	*Scarf or Stole at Ordination? A Plea for the Evangelical Conscience*	Andrew Atherstone
LB11	*How to Write a Theology Essay*	Michael P. Jensen
LB12	*Preaching: A Guidebook for Beginners*	Allan Chapple
LB13	*Justification by Faith: Orientating the Church's teaching and practice to Christ (Toon Lecture 1)*	Michael Nazir-Ali
LB14	*"Remember Your Leaders": Principles and Priorities for Leaders from Hebrews 13*	Wallace Benn
LB15	*How the Anglican Communion came to be and where it is going*	Michael Nazir-Ali
LB16	*Divine Allurement: Cranmer's Comfortable Words*	Ashley Null
LB17	*True Devotion: In Search of Authentic Spirituality*	Allan Chapple
LB18	*Commemorating War and Praying for Peace: A Christian reflection on the Armed Forces*	John Neal

Anglican Foundations Series

FWC	*The Faith We Confess: An Exposition of the 39 Articles*	Gerald Bray
AF02	*The 'Very Pure Word of God': The Book of Common Prayer as a Model of Biblical Liturgy*	Peter Adam
AF03	*Dearly Beloved: Building God's People Through Morning and Evening Prayer*	Mark Burkill
AF04	*Day by Day: The Rhythm of the Bible in the Book of Common Prayer*	Benjamin Sargent
AF05	*The Supper: Cranmer and Communion*	Nigel Scotland
AF06	*A Fruitful Exhortation: A Guide to the Homilies*	Gerald Bray
AF07	*Instruction in the Way of the Lord: A Guide to the Prayer Book Catechism*	Martin Davie
AF08	*Till Death Us Do Part: "The Solemnization of Matrimony" in the Book of Common Prayer*	Simon Vibert
AF09	*'Sure and Certain Hope': Death and Burial in the Book of Common Prayer*	Andrew Cinnamond

Latimer Publications

Latimer Books

GGC	*God, Gays and the Church: Human Sexuality and Experience in Christian Thinking*	eds. Lisa Nolland, Chris Sugden, Sarah Finch
WTL	*The Way, the Truth and the Life: Theological Resources for a Pilgrimage to a Global Anglican Future*	eds. Vinay Samuel, Chris Sugden, Sarah Finch
AEID	*Anglican Evangelical Identity – Yesterday and Today*	J.I.Packer, N.T.Wright
IB	*The Anglican Evangelical Doctrine of Infant Baptism*	John Stott, Alec Motyer
BF	*Being Faithful: The Shape of Historic Anglicanism Today*	Theological Resource Group of GAFCON
TPG	*The True Profession of the Gospel: Augustus Toplady and Reclaiming our Reformed Foundations*	Lee Gatiss
SG	*Shadow Gospel: Rowan Williams and the Anglican Communion Crisis*	Charles Raven
TTB	*Translating the Bible: From William Tyndale to King James*	Gerald Bray
PWS	*Pilgrims, Warriors, and Servants: Puritan Wisdom for Today's Church*	ed. Lee Gatiss
PPA	*Preachers, Pastors, and Ambassadors: Puritan Wisdom for Today's Church*	ed. Lee Gatiss
CWP	*The Church, Women Bishops and Provision: The Integrity of Orthodox Objections to the Proposed Legislation Allowing Women Bishops*	
TSF	*The Truth Shall Set You Free: Global Anglicans in the 21st Century*	ed. Charles Raven
LMM	*Launching Marsden's Mission: The Beginnings of the Church Missionary Society in New Zealand, viewed from New South Wales*	eds. Peter G Bolt, David B. Pettett
MST1	*Listen To Him: Reading and Preaching Emmanuel in Matthew*	ed. Peter Bolt
GWC	*The Genius of George Whitefield: Reflections on his Ministry from 21st Century Africa*	eds. Benjamin Dean & Adriaan Neele
MLD2	*From Cambridge to Colony: Charles Simeon's Enduring Influence on Christianity in Australia*	ed. Edward Loane

Lightning Source UK Ltd.
Milton Keynes UK
UKOW04f1623210216

268751UK00001BA/9/P

9 781906 327392